PATHFINDER HISTORY

The Crusades

Irene Merrall

Series Historical Consultant:
Dr R. A. H. Robinson,
The University of Birmingham

Stanley Thornes (Publishers) Ltd

First published in 1999 by:
Stanley Thornes (Publishers) Ltd
Ellenborough House
Wellington Street
CHELTENHAM GL50 1YW
England

99 00 01 02 03/ 10 9 8 7 6 5 4 3 2 1

A catalogue record for this book is available from the British Library.

ISBN 0-7487-4343-X

Typeset by Tech-Set Ltd, Gateshead, Tyne & Wear
Illustrated by Davide Provenzale
Cover photograph: The British Library
Picture research by Christina Morgan
Printed and bound in Great Britain by Redwood Books, Trowbridge, Wiltshire

Acknowledgements

With thanks to the following for permission to reproduce photographs in this book:

Bridgeman Art Library, London/Bibliothèque Nationale, Paris, page 39
British Library Reproductions, pages 18, 21, 45
Explorer, Paris/René Lanaud, page 31
RMN, Paris/Musée du Chateau, Versailles, page 9
Roger-Viollet, Paris, page 33

Every effort has been made to contact copyright holders. The publishers apologise to anyone whose rights have been inadvertently overlooked, and will be happy to rectify any errors or omissions.

Contents

How to Use this Book   4

SECTION 1   OVERVIEW

The Big Picture   6

The Key Issues   10

Information: Where to Find it and How to Use it   12

SECTION 2   ENQUIRY AND INVESTIGATION

Chapter 1 East and West on the Eve of the Crusades   14
   – Western Europe in the 11th Century   14
   – The East in the 11th Century   16

Chapter 2 The Causes of the First Crusade   18
   – Pope Urban's Appeal   18
   – The Response of the Knights   20

Chapter 3 The Course of the First Crusade   22
   – The Journey Begins   22
   – Towards Jerusalem   24

Chapter 4 Crusader States and Society   26
   – The Founding of the Crusader States   26
   – The Influence of the West   28

Chapter 5 The Military Orders   30
   – The Beginnings   30
   – The Development of the Orders   32

Chapter 6 The Muslim Recovery   34
   – Zengi and Nureddin   34
   – Saladin   36

Chapter 7 The Second Crusade   38
   – A Crusade Led by Kings   38
   – A Debacle in Outremer   40

Chapter 8 The Third Crusade   42
   – A New Crusade   42
   – Richard and Saladin   44

Chapter 9 The Fourth Crusade   46
   – Complications and Diversions   46
   – The Attack on Constantinople   48

SECTION 3   REVIEW

Synthesis: The Crusading Ideal   50

Argument   54

Final Review   60

Index   64

How to Use this Book

History at A-level is a more complex and demanding subject than at any preceding level, and it is with these new and higher demands on students in mind that the Pathfinder History series has been written. The basic aim of the book is simple: to enable you to appreciate the important issues that lie behind the crusades.

What this book does not do is provide a single source of all the answers needed for exam success. The very nature of A-level study demands that you use a range of resources in your studies, in order to build up the understanding of different interpretations on issues, and develop your own argument on exam topics. Pathfinder can make this subject more accessible by defining the key issues, giving an initial understanding of them and helping you to define questions for further investigation. It concentrates on the fundamentals surrounding the crusades, and the important issues, events and other characters of the period that you must understand, and which the examiners will want to see that you know.

Hence it becomes more of a guide book to the subject, and can be used whenever you want within the A-level course; as an introduction, as a reminder revision text or throughout the course each time a new topic is started. Pathfinder also has several important features to help you get to grips with the crusades and their context.

The book follows the three basic stages of the A-level process, explaining why they are important and why you are doing them. The three sections of the book are thus Overview, Enquiry and Investigation, and Review. These describe the three main methods of studying History at A-level; so, for example, when you answer a question on the causes of the first crusade, you will recall why this book approaches this topic with these three headings in mind.

KEY ISSUES AND KEY SKILLS

Pathfinder is written around three basic principles. The first is that it covers the most important events, themes, ideas and concepts of the subject, called the *Key Issues*. The second is that there are levels or tiers to these issues, so that a major question is broken down into its contributory questions and issues and is thus easier to understand. And the third principle is that there are fundamental skills that you must develop and employ as historians at this level, and these are referred to as the *Key Skills*.

These principles combine in Section 1, where **The Big Picture** sets the whole scene of the topic, and identifies the most important periods and events within the topic. What **The Key Issues** does is to establish what the author believes are the fundamental questions and answers to the subject as a whole, and then examine these in more detail by raising contributory questions contained within the main question. Each period is discussed in more detail in Section 2, and you will see page references for each appropriate chapter. Each period thus has its own issues and concepts, to provide a second tier of Key Issues. Finally, the **Information: Where to Find it and How to Use it** section offers hints and advice on the active study skills you will be using in A-level History.

The main focus of the book is Section 2, called **Enquiry and Investigation** because this is exactly what you are being asked to do for most of the time during the A-level process. You are making historical enquiries and learning how to interpret sources and information every time you look at a document, analyse a photograph or read around a topic. Each chapter takes as its title one of the periods identified in The Big Picture, and each one also identifies what you need to bear in mind when working on that particular issue or theme.

There is a useful little tab at the start of each spread which summarises the most important aspects of the topic and identifies the skills that you will need to use when studying it. These are the Key Skills, although you could think of them as key study skills if you prefer. There are a number of them and they can be grouped together in the following headings with these definitions:

Skills for collecting information from historical sources

- Analysis: breaking down information into component parts (making notes under section headings, for example).
- Interpretation: considering the implications of information and cross-referencing to other sources or contextual knowledge to develop your understanding further. (Skills used within this are actually inference, deduction, extrapolation, interpolation, recall and synthesis.)
- Evaluation: assessing the validity of sources and hence the implications for the reliability of the information that they provide.
- Recording: arranging information into sections that allow easy retrieval when required. For example, making linear notes (good for large amounts of information), diagrams and flow-charts or mind maps (good for establishing relationships between sections of information).

Skills for applying and using information

- Explanation: using information to show how and why something happened.
- Assessment: weighing up possible explanations or interpretations.
- Forming hypotheses: setting up an explanation or judgement for further testing.
- Testing hypotheses: using information to support and challenge a hypothesis to improve it.
- Setting a thesis: using the information to present, support and sustain a tested hypothesis and an explanation of historical processes.

You will see that some skills are flagged more often than others, and there may be others that are not defined here. However, the important point to remember is that these are the skills that the A-level historian has to have available for use, and that you are actually using them all the time already. The aim is to reinforce these skills for you, and to enable you to see how you are using them and why.

Section 3 **Review** then brings all the interpretations, investigations and issues that you have looked at on the crusades into one place. **Synthesis** is the bringing together of issues, arguments and judgements into overall answers. It also poses answers as to what the author considers to be the main issues identified in Section 1. **Argument** then takes the information and hypotheses and applies them to more detailed essay answers, of the style you might find or that you might write in the exam. The **Final Review** is something of the author's own thoughts and conclusions to the subject on a broad level.

MARGINS AND ICONS

Pathfinder divides material as part of the main aim of focusing attention on the most important issues. Hence the main central narrative discusses and interprets information and, although detailed, cannot provide all the information on its topic. It can be integrated with and supplemented by more detailed books, articles and documents.

All other sorts of information appear in the margins and you will see the following icons used alongside them. Not all icons appear in every chapter and some chapters have other features included as well, but the icons should help you manage the extra information given on topics.

 Documents, historiography and sources – quotes from texts, individuals and passages

 Suggested headings for notes

 Suggested further reading

 Sample activities and exam-style questions

 General hints, study tips and advice

Key terms

What were the crusades?

The word 'crusade' is commonly used these days when people join together to promote a particular cause, in which they believe wholeheartedly. The word comes from the Latin *crux*, which means a cross. The original crusaders were people from western Europe who went off to fight in the Holy Land, and wore a cross on their clothes to show that they were fighting for Christ. The English word 'crusade', however, was not invented until the 18th century. There were eight crusades to the Holy Land; in this book we shall be concerned mainly with the first four.

The daughter of Alexius Comnenus saw the crusaders as they approached Constantinople in 1096:

'Full of enthusiasm and ardour, they thronged every highway, and with these warriors came a host of civilians ... carrying palms and bearing crosses on their shoulders. There were women and children too, who had left their own countries. Like tributaries joining a river from all directions they streamed towards us in full force.'

The Big Picture

EUROPE AND THE EAST IN THE 11TH CENTURY

- The whole of western Europe was of the Roman Catholic faith and recognised the pope in Rome as its head. Society was turbulent. Kings were weak and knights were at war with each other over the land that they needed to support themselves.
- Between 1077 and 1092 the pope had been in dispute with the Holy Roman emperor, Henry IV, and had allied himself with the Normans, who ruled southern Italy and Sicily.
- Eastern Europe was part of the Byzantine empire, which was of the Greek Orthodox faith. The Byzantine empire had lost lands to the Normans in southern Italy and to the Seljuk Turks in Asia Minor (modern Turkey). In 1081 Alexius Comnenus became emperor and sought the opportunity to regain his territory.
- The lands of Islam formed the other major civilisation and its forces had occupied most of the near east and southern Spain. In the 1090s the Seljuk Turks fell out with each other and their lands became divided.

THE FIRST CRUSADE

- In 1095 Alexius Comnenus appealed to the pope in Rome for help.
- The pope, Urban II, at the Council of Clermont, called for Christian knights to answer the call and go to the rescue of the Holy Land. Others also preached the cause and many responded.
- In 1096 Peter the Hermit led a force across Europe towards Constantinople, the Byzantine capital. They were convinced that it was God's will that they should kill the enemies of Christ; they began by massacring the Jews who inhabited the cities through which they passed. They were ferried across the Bosphorus by Alexius Comnenus and were wiped out by the Turks near Nicaea.
- In 1097 a second wave, this time led by led by important knights and the pope's representative, reached the Holy Land via Constantinople. They defeated the Muslims at Niceaea and Dorylaeum, took Edessa and Antioch and made their way to Jerusalem.
- In 1099 Jerusalem was captured and its inhabitants massacred while the crusaders rejoiced and gave praise to God.

THE LATIN STATES (OUTREMER)

- Some of the crusaders made their homes in the east. Antioch and Edessa became the first of what were known as the Latin states (sometimes called Outremer). The capture of Tripoli in 1109 completed their formation.
- After the capture of Jerusalem, Godfrey de Bouillon was elected as its ruler. He took the title Defender of the Holy Sepulchre but his successors were known as the kings of Jerusalem.

- The success of the first crusade gave it a spiritual significance because it was believed that God had made the Christians victorious. The Latin states became a concern of western Christendom. The Christian, or Frankish, population of the Latin states was never large enough to defend itself adequately.
- The Italian cities of Venice, Genoa and Pisa brought supplies by sea and were granted important privileges in the ports. This enabled them to build up their power and influence.
- Lands were not returned to the Byzantine empire and the relationship between the crusaders and successive emperors became increasingly strained and embittered.

THE MILITARY ORDERS

- In order to protect crusader territory, two orders of monks, who were also knights, were founded – the Knights of the Temple of Solomon (the Templars) and the Knights of St John of Jerusalem (the Hospitallers).
- They came to embody the crusading ideal – a physical warrior, fighting against the enemies of Christ, who was the equivalent of the spiritual warrior, the monk, waging war against the forces of evil in his monastery.
- They were supported financially by gifts of money and land in the west and became a standing army of dedicated professional soldiers.
- They built castles along the frontiers and took over castles from knights who could no longer afford to maintain them because of the economic situation in the Holy Land.
- Their wealth enabled them to act independently. This caused problems with the kings of Jerusalem and the commanders of armies in the Latin states.

THE MUSLIM RECOVERY

- The Muslim forces who had attacked the crusaders of the first crusade were disunited. They were waging war against each other and underestimated the threat from the west.
- After their defeats in 1097–1099 they began to regroup and unite. There were three outstanding Muslim leaders who brought this about – Zengi, Nureddin and Saladin.
- In 1144 Zengi, the atabeg (ruler) of Mosul, conquered Edessa and then all the non-Frankish states in Syria. He won the approval of the caliph of Baghdad and his battles were identified as part of a holy war, or jihad.
- Nureddin, Zengi's son, developed the idea of the jihad and conquered the Muslim country of Egypt in order to use its wealth to further his campaigns.
- Saladin united the Egyptian Muslims (Fatimids) with the Abbasid dynasty in Baghdad. He set about uniting the dominions of Nureddin in Syria with Egypt. To do this he had to wage war on the Latin states, which lay in between these two areas.

Pope – The supreme leader of the Roman Catholic church in western Europe

Holy Roman emperor – the king of the largest European country, which included modern Germany. The Holy Roman empire dated back to AD 800 when Charlemagne was crowned emperor by the pope, reviving the idea of the ancient Roman empire.

Byzantine empire – the eastern part of the Roman empire. The Byzantine emperor was also head of the Greek Orthodox church in the east.

Seljuk Turks – a nomadic race of people from central Asia, converts to Islam and excellent warriors, who had conquered most of the Muslim world in the east

Islam – the religion founded by the Arab prophet Mohammed (570–632)

Near east – the area around the eastern shores of the Mediterranean sea

Holy Land – the land described in the Bible: modern day Israel and part of Syria

Peter the Hermit – a poor preacher from Amiens in France

Godfrey de Bouillon – the duke of Lower Lorraine, leader of the northern French and Rhinelander contingent of the crusade

Franks – those who settled in the Latin states. Most were from the land of the Franks, i.e. modern France, although some were from Italy and what is now Germany. Frankish is the adjective often used to describe the Latin states or its inhabitants.

Muslim – a follower of the religion of Islam

Caliph – a successor of Mohammed (literally 'deputy of the Prophet'). The caliph was a religious and a political leader.

Jihad – a holy war against unbelievers.

The poetry of war

With numberless rich
    pennons streaming
And flags and banners of fair
    seeming
Then thirty thousand Turkish
    troops
And more, ranged in well
    ordered groups,
Garbed and accoutred
    splendidly,
Dashed on the host impetuously.
Like lightning speed their
    horses fleet,
And dust rose thick before their
    feet.

By Ambroise,
a Norman minstrel

Abbasid and Fatimid dynasties – Islam had its divisions, as did Christianity. The Abbasid dynasty ruled from Baghdad. They were Sunnites, who believed that the first three caliphs who had followed Mohammed were the true ones. The Fatimid dynasty ruled from Cairo. They were Shi'ites, who believed that the fourth caliph and his descendants were the only true ones.

Bernard of Clairvaux – the abbot of Clairvaux in France, one of the most respected and influential churchmen in Europe and a gifted preacher

Innocent III – pope from 1198 to 1216, a very strong and practical man who claimed the right to interfere in secular matters

Doge – the ruler of Venice was known as the doge

THE SECOND CRUSADE

- The western nations were shocked by the fall of Edessa to the Muslims in 1144 and a second crusade was preached.
- The second crusade was led by kings – Louis VII of France and Conrad III of Germany. They had been inspired to take the cross by the persuasive preaching of Bernard of Clairvaux.
- On the face of it this crusade looked more powerful than the first. However, there was no overall leader and there was conflict between the western knights, with high religious ideals, and those who lived in the east, who understood the local conditions.
- In 1148 matters came to a head at Damascus, which was beseiged against the advice of the eastern knights. The crusaders abandoned a good position with water in the orchards near the city for a position near a less well defended area. Within a few days they were forced to admit defeat. The second crusade was a failure.

THE THIRD CRUSADE

- As the Muslims became more united under strong leadership, and inspired by the idea of the jihad, so the Christians became more divided and weakened by disputes about the succession to the throne of Jerusalem and quarrels between the eastern and western knights.
- In 1187 the forces of Saladin inflicted a crushing blow to the Frankish army at Hattin and then went on to reconquer Jerusalem.
- The reconquest of Jerusalem, the holy city, caused great consternation in the west and Pope Gregory VIII proclaimed a third crusade. This crusade was again led by kings, this time by Frederick Barbarossa of Germany, Philip II (Augustus) of France and Richard I (the Lionheart) of England.
- Frederick Barbarossa was drowned in 1190. Richard and Philip Augustus secured the port of Acre for the crusaders and then Philip returned to France in 1191, after only a few months campaigning.
- Richard the Lionheart gained a reputation as a great warrior leader and the respect of his enemy Saladin. He won a great victory at Arsuf in 1191 but failed to regain Jerusalem. He had to return to the west in order to deal with problems in his own empire, but he had secured a port and this enabled the Latin states to struggle on.

THE FOURTH CRUSADE

- In 1198 Pope Innocent III called for another crusade. This time no kings responded.
- The crusaders assembled in Venice, from where they were to go by sea to the Holy Land. They were promised their passage if they helped the doge of Venice to take the Christian town of Zara on the Adriatic sea. The pope tried to prevent the crusaders from attacking it but without success.
- The crusaders then went to Constantinople to support the claim of Alexius Angelus in a dynastic struggle for the Byzantine throne.
- After only a few months Alexius was killed and the crusaders captured and sacked the city of Constantinople.
- The former Byzantine empire was split into fiefs and shared amongst the crusaders, who abandoned their plans for going to the Holy Land.

A 19th-century painting of Richard the Lionheart and Philip Augustus capturing a city in the Holy Land

Crusade chronology

1095 Pope Urban II proclaims the first crusade

1099 The capture of Jerusalem and the setting up of the Latin (Crusader) states

1144 The Seljuk Turks capture Edessa and Bernard of Clairvaux preaches the second crusade

1147–9 The second crusade fails

1187 The Frankish army is defeated at Hattin. Muslim forces, under Saladin, reconquer Jerusalem

1189–92 The third crusade, which secures Acre but fails to recapture Jerusalem

1202–4 The fourth crusade: the sack of Constantinople and the setting up of a Latin empire there

1217–21 The fifth crusade: the capture of Damietta in Egypt, which is soon lost

1228–9 The sixth crusade: the emperor Frederick II recaptures Jerusalem and is crowned king. Islam retakes Jerusalem in 1244

1248–50 The seventh crusade: Louis IX of France is taken prisoner in Egypt and goes on pilgrimage to Jerusalem

1270 The eighth crusade: Louis IX leads the crusade against Tunis and dies there

1291 The Mamluk Turks capture Acre, the last foothold of the Latin states

An extremely clear and comprehensive description of the world at this time is Trevor John, *East and West at the Time of the Crusades* (Ginn & Co., 1972). It was written for secondary school pupils but is, unfortunately, out of print. It would be worthwhile trying to track down a copy through inter-library loan.

What are Key Issues?

When we study history we first of all want to find out what happened. We need to know the story. You may have noticed, however, that the books you are reading on the crusades rarely tell a straightforward story. This is because individual historians are selecting evidence, interpreting it, trying to explain why they interpret it in a certain way and, sometimes, why they disagree with other historians. This can be very difficult to understand at first. The Key Issues help you by identifying some of the important areas and the questions that need to be asked. This should enable you to read the history books in a different way. If you are looking for answers to specific questions, then you are making your own selection in order to find the answers. You are less likely to get lost or confused in the many points that the historian is putting forward, and more able to compare one historian's point of view with another and come to your own conclusions.

The Key Issues are also the 'what', 'how' or 'why' questions that underlie the type of questions that you will get in your examinations. It is important, at A-level, to do some deep thinking before you get into the examination room. You need to try to understand how people thought in the past, why they did what they did, as well as what happened. If you understand the Key Issues you will have done some serious thinking and will have a good understanding. It will then be much easier in an examination to relate the knowledge that you have to the question on the paper.

The Key Issues

THE ROLE OF RELIGION

The world of the crusaders is very far removed from our own. It was a world where religion, rather than race or nationality, was the factor by which people identified themselves. The Christian world was divided into the Latin of the Roman Catholic church in the west, and the Greek of the church of the Byzantine empire in the east. Society in western Europe was feudal, brutal and coarse. In the east it was more cultured and sophisticated but warfare was common to both. The first thing we shall do in this book is to look more closely at the world in which the first crusaders lived, to see the forces at work that led to this huge involvement of Europe with the affairs of the near east. To do this we shall look, in the first two chapters, at the place that religion held in the hearts and minds of 11th-century people.

We shall also investigate the motives of the first crusaders. The pope called for the crusade and we need to look at why he did this. Was it to support his brethren in the Greek Orthodox faith, or to be acknowledged as the supreme leader in Christendom, or was he trying to find a role for the numbers of landless knights that were constantly fighting each other? The eastern and western churches had separated in 1054, the rulers of Byzantium had been at war with the Normans in Sicily and southern Italy, and there was an atmosphere of distrust between the two churches. We need to look also, therefore, at what the Byzantine emperor was hoping to achieve by appealing to the west for help.

A PILGRIMAGE IN ARMS

The first crusaders lacked leadership, organisation, resources and supplies. It is incredible that any of them reached the Holy Land at all, and yet they managed to capture Jerusalem. A key issue is why the first crusade was successful against all the odds. We shall examine what part the supernatural played in this, and compare it with the role played by the different personalities, and especially the aid given by the Byzantine emperor. The success of the first crusade and the way this was interpreted may have led to the development of a crusading ideal and a sense of responsiblity for the welfare of the Holy Land. How did the success of this crusade affect those that followed? We shall address this question in chapter 3.

THE CRUSADER STATES

The capture of Jerusalem meant that the crusaders were able to form the Latin states in the east, but there were never enough Frankish, or western, Christians living there to reproduce the kind of society that they had known in the west. What kind of society was established there and what was its relationship with the west? We shall look at this question in chapter 4. Some kind of compromise with the people living around them was necessary in order to exist at all, but they were not assimilated into the eastern way of life. How, then, did the crusader states manage to exist for so long? There were many factors involved in the survival of the Latin states: the Italian cities brought supplies and provided the protection of a fleet; forces from the west came to help in times of crisis and nobles from the west came to marry their princesses and become their kings. However, for every positive aspect of support from the west there was a negative aspect, and we shall need to evaluate the importance of all these factors. A key issue is the defence of the Holy Land. There was a constant need for defence and yet there were never enough knights to provide it effectively. The founding of the military orders helped to provide a standing army: what was their role in maintaining the Latin states? We shall consider this question in chapter 5.

The Forces of Islam

If the first crusade succeeded against the odds, the second failed despite the leadership of kings and the backing of one of the greatest religious leaders of the day. What factors led to its failure? One difference was that the Muslims had managed to draw together and unite in a sacred cause. How were they able to do this, and how far did the crusades themselves encourage Muslim unity? We shall look at these issues in chapters 6 and 7,

The Third Crusade

In chapter 8 we shall see that the third crusade failed to recapture Jerusalem, the centre of the world in Christian eyes. Richard I was left in sole command of the crusader forces and gained a great reputation as a warrior, but he actually failed to achieve his goal. He turned back from attacking Jeruslem in order to save the ports and he had to return home to deal with problems caused by his absence. In view of this, what was the significance of the third crusade?

A Change of Direction

In our last chapter in the enquiry and investigation section we shall see that there was a change of direction in more ways than one. The fourth crusade did not go to the Holy Land. The crusaders sacked Constantinople and carved up the Byzantine empire between them. In 1095 the west had responded to a plea from the Byzantine emperor; in 1204 they had sacked his capital city and established their own empire. How and why did the fourth crusade differ so much from those that had taken place earlier? What had happened to the crusading ideal? What forces were now at work?

The crusading ideal

The issue of a crusading ideal continues through the story of the crusades. An ideal is something that is perfect, or a model to follow. It can only exist in the imagination because nothing that is real is perfect. When historians talk about a crusading ideal, therefore, they mean the idea of a perfect crusade that existed in the minds of people who wrote at the time.

As we have little written evidence, it is difficult to find out what the majority of people may have been thinking. We have to remember that most of the writers from the west were monks. They wrote about the events of the crusades and created the ideal. Their lives were spent in the study of the Bible and in prayer. They interpreted events in a religious way and, consequently, the ideal was a religious one. There were many changes in the church during the 11th and 12th centuries, including changes in thinking. The ideal of the crusade also changed, therefore, and we will consider how this happened in the synthesis section at the end of this book.

What is a crusade?

Many recent authors take a wider view of what the crusades were, and they write about other wars as well as those in the near east that are covered in this book. A look at the contents page will generally show you what topics the author is going to cover. It is important to know and understand the views of different historians but it can be a little confusing at first if you don't understand that there are different definitions of a crusade.

Inter-library loan

For a very small fee, usually less than £1, your local library will find a copy of any book that you ask for. Sometimes it will take quite a time to find the book that you want but often it can be done within a couple of weeks. Some of the works recommended in this book are out of print. This means that you would not be able to buy them, but your local library would be able to track down a copy for you to borrow.

Tape recordings

Sussex Publications Ltd, 2–6 Foscote Mews, London W9 2HH have produced a tape-recorded discussion between Professor Joan Hussey and Dr R. C. Smail on the crusades and Byzantium. It is very interesting and informative to hear two historians discussing their views.

Information: Where to Find it and How to Use it

SOURCES

Sources for history in this period are limited. Obviously there were no photographs, newspaper reports or films made at this time, but there were also very few pictures of any kind. Most of the primary sources were written by churchmen, as they were the only people in the western world who could read or write. It is unlikely that new primary sources will be found for you to use, but there are many secondary sources, or interpretations of the existing sources, and historians are constantly seeking new ways of analysing the information that is available.

BOOKS

Books are going to be your main source of information. Books are written with a particular audience, or readership, in mind. Decide first of all what kind of audience you are. At first you will probably be a reader who is new to the topic and who wants a general overview in simple terms, so that you can identify what happened when and who was involved. Later on you will want to read about certain aspects in more detail, to compare the views of different historians and to find out why these things happened.

Start with the books that give an overview. You will probably find some Key Stage 3 books on medieval realms which have a section on the crusades. There are also some very good older books, such as those in the Focus on History series. As the national curriculum encourages the chronological study of history the Key Stage 3 books will be written for younger pupils, but do not ignore them because of this. Just as watching the news programme on children's TV can often give you a good understanding of issues behind the news, so reading books written for younger pupils can give you a good idea of what was important in a period. For adults, general histories of the period give an overview. It is a good idea to read the sections on the crusades completely, making brief summary notes.

When you have a good understanding of the main events and personalities you will then need to move on to more detailed books, or books on different aspects of the topic. You will probably be provided with books and a reading list by your teacher. Get into the habit of looking at bibliographies in the back of books to see what else might be useful. For the most part, if you are trying to find information, you will not need to read whole books. The introduction and conclusion are very important chapters as they will tell you the main thrust of the author's argument. The contents page and index are also very useful tools. Flick through to see if a book has information that you need to answer a particular question. Read as widely as you possibly can and you will find that you will become very familiar with the events and personalities. You will also start to see where historians agree and disagree with each other.

GEOGRAPHY IS IMPORTANT

You will find that an ordinary atlas will be extremely helpful in the study of the crusades. Geography and history are very closely related. Not only will an atlas help you to know where places are, or were, but also you will find details of the climate and the physical features that made so much difference to the people moving to and living in the east. An historical atlas is also a very useful tool.

TECHNOLOGY

CD ROM encyclopaedias are very useful for an overview of the main events and for short biographies of the main personalities. They are easy to read because they are written for a large audience with a general interest. The depth and detail will be limited, however, and they do not cover the different points of view of historians. They will recommend books for further reading and they may give picture sources. If you have access to the Internet, it is worthwhile seeing what information is available there. Always remember, though, that information itself is of limited value. You have to read, analyse and interpret it, however you obtain it, and you can spend hours 'surfing the net' only to find that in the end you have the same information in the book that is lying on the desk beside your computer.

Television programmes and films help to give a visual picture of the landscape, the conditions that the crusaders endured and their buildings, as well as a sense of the drama of the period. Look out for programmes on the crusades or biographies of the personalities involved. If you have access to satellite or cable TV, the History Channel sometimes shows programmes that are relevant to this topic. We have to remember, however, that even television programmes that show us the actual terrain over which the crusaders walked are the programme maker's interpretation of the available sources. We should always try to evaluate the sources of information.

READING AND WRITING

Reading and writing are closely connected. While you are reading for information, consider that the book you have been reading has been written by a real person. He or she would have had to collect and interpret the evidence, work out a point of view and then put it over in a piece of writing. A great deal of research, thinking, planning, drafting and redrafting will have gone into your book. Occasionally, instead of focusing on the information you have been seeking, it is worth considering the way in which the author practises the craft of writing. We can often learn by seeing how other people do things. Ask yourself what exactly authors are doing in an introduction. Are they defining terms or setting the scene? How do they move from one paragraph to another? How do they bring their work to a conclusion? Can you get back to what their plan must have been by reading the first sentence of each paragraph? Are there any useful phrases that recur that you could use yourself for specific purposes, such as linking or reviewing? This will help you when you take notes, because you will learn what are the essentials that you need to note down, and it will help you to improve your own writing.

Videos

The BBC has produced a series of documentaries on the first three crusades. Terry Jones follows in the footsteps of the crusaders and manages to put over the horror of the crusades at the same time as entertaining his audience by interpreting some events in a comic light. The series, called *Crusades*, was produced in 1995 by BBC/A & E Network (producer Alan Ereira, director David Wallace).

Taking notes

If you are reading generally, with no specific questions in mind, take minimal notes, perhaps just of chapter headings and the subjects dealt with in a particular book. You can then always go back to it if you need to research something in more detail. A specific question to answer will focus your reading and lead you to take notes in a different way.

If you write on one side of your paper only, you can then cut up your notes and sort information in preparation for writing essays. It is also a good idea to keep a record of quotable quotes, possibly on cards that can be filed under different headings and cross referenced. Always remember to record the full title of the book, the author and the relevant page number, as you will need to refer to it if you use the quote in your own writing.

THE KEY ISSUE

● What forces were at work in western Europe in 1095 that may have led to the crusades?

THE KEY SKILLS

Analysis
Explanation
Assessment
Recording

Relic – the remains of, or an object connected with, Jesus Christ or one of the saints, for example part of the cross on which Jesus was crucified, or the bones of a saint

Penance – a harsh action imposed by a priest in order to show sorrow for sin and to obtain forgiveness

Pilgrimage – a journey to a shrine or holy place to seek forgiveness of sins, healing, help in trouble, or to give thanks to God

Knight – a mounted warrior. Knights had their own code of honour and behaviour (chivalry).

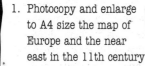

1. Photocopy and enlarge to A4 size the map of Europe and the near east in the 11th century

2. Shade the Christian areas in a colour of your choice and make a key.

3. Annotate the map with the names of the rulers and a summary of their situation. This will act as a point of reference for you.

Western Europe in the 11th Century

THE STRUGGLE FOR SURVIVAL

In order to understand why the crusades happened, we must try to understand the world in which the crusaders lived. Perhaps the easiest way to do this is to look at the 11th-century world as a series of struggles of one kind or another. The first struggle was common to everyone – the struggle to survive. Western Europe was underpopulated and only a fraction of the land was cultivated. Food shortages, famine, disease and early death were common. There was little comfort but the hope of a better life to come after death, and it is not surprising that religion held an important place in the hearts and minds of medieval people. Apart from southern Spain, which was Muslim, and certain areas north of the Baltic sea, which were pagan, western Europe was Christian, which in that part of the world meant it followed the Roman Catholic faith.

THE STRUGGLE FOR SALVATION

For Christians, although a place in heaven was reserved for the righteous, the punishment for sinners was eternal damnation in hell. The second struggle, therefore, was that of good against evil. The aim of the good was salvation: to have sins forgiven and to gain a place in heaven. The most certain way of obtaining salvation was to become a monk or nun – to leave the world and fight the battle against the forces of evil in prayer. It was thought that God listened to the prayers of monks and nuns on behalf of others. The relics of saints were also thought to have a special significance, and a pilgrimage to one of the major shrines in Europe could be made as a penance, in order to gain forgiveness for past sins. The most important place of pilgrimage was Jerusalem, where Jesus Christ had been crucified and had risen from the dead. There, even the stones of the buildings were considered to be holy relics.

THE STRUGGLE FOR SUPREMACY

The structure of society was what has been called 'feudal'. That is, men held land in return for swearing an oath to serve and advise their lord, who, in turn, swore to give them his protection. Society was organised around the need to fight. The nobility were knights, trained to their calling from boyhood. Kings were weak and struggled to establish their right to rule. A kingdom was only that area in which a king could physically enforce his authority. In France, this meant that the king ruled only the area around Paris. In the rest of his lands local lords fought him, each other and the church for control of the land that they needed to support themselves and their horses. There was little organised law and order. There were few luxuries and refinements of life.

THE STRUGGLE OF EMPEROR AND POPE

The largest European country was the German, or Holy Roman, Empire. In Germany, the emperors had gained control by appointing churchmen as their representatives. In the past, the emperor had also appointed popes. From the middle of the 11th century there had been important reforms in the church. Popes had insisted that they had control over the election of bishops and that all Christendom, including emperors and kings, were their subjects. The German emperor, Henry IV, had been in dispute with the pope since 1076. Effectively the emperor and the pope were struggling for control of western Christendom.

THE STRUGGLE IN SOUTHERN ITALY

In Normandy there there were many highly trained knights, more than could be used in the wars of the Norman dukes. Many of these knights were younger sons who were looking for other wars to fight and other lands to conquer and settle. From the early 11th century the Normans had been engaged in a struggle in southern Italy, where the Italian noblemen and the armies of the Muslims and the Byzantines were all trying to gain control. In order to help them in their struggle against the German emperors, the popes had turned to the Normans in southern Italy. In 1095 the emperor was in a weak position, the pope, Urban II, in a strong one. If he could mobilise the forces of Christendom on a mission of his choosing then he could prove beyond doubt that the pope was the supreme leader – that the church was superior to the state.

Europe and the near east in the 11th century

Who was who in Europe in 1095?

Italy – the pope was Urban II, a Frenchman who understood the situation in Northern France

England – William Rufus was king. His brother, Robert Curthose, was Duke of Normandy. William wanted Normandy. He had quarrelled with the pope.

Southern Italy – Norman Robert Guiscard and his younger brother, Roger, had taken Sicily from the Muslims in 1091 to add to the duchies of Apulia and Calabria, already under Norman rule.

France – Philip I was king. A very weak monarch, he had been excommunicated by the pope.

Germany – In 1095 Henry IV had been excommunicated by the pope, and German counts and barons had taken advantage of the situation to rebel against him

Spain – Spain was divided into three Christian kingdoms in the north and many Arab principalities in the south. Christians were fighting to regain lost territory. The leader of this movement was Alphonso VI of Castile. The pope supported campaigns against the Muslims and had promised forgiveness of their sins for those who took part.

Any of the texts that you have on the crusades will have introductory chapters setting the scene. You need to read and make notes on them. Use the headings of this chapter to help you analyse what you are reading: you can also use them as headings for your notes.

Find out, from whatever sources are available, about the Roman Catholic church and its beliefs.

THE KEY ISSUE

● What forces were at work in the east in 1095 that may have led to the crusades?

THE KEY SKILLS

Analysis

Explanation

Assessment

Recording

Forming hypotheses

Excommunication– expulsion from the Christian church

Dynasty – a succession of rulers of the same family

Sultan – a Muslim ruler

Emirate – a Muslim state

Atabeg – literally 'prince-father', a Muslim ruler or high official

What forces were at work in 1095 that led to the crusades? **?**

To answer this question you will need to identify the major factors. In this case, these might be economic and social problems, religious differences, political struggles and rivalries between church and state. You need to organise your information and put together a logical and reasoned answer.

1. Find out about the Greek Orthodox church and how its doctrines, organisation and methods of worship differ from the Roman Catholic church. **?**
2. Find out about the Muslim faith. How does it differ from Christianity?

The East in the 11th Century

THE BYZANTINE STRUGGLE AGAINST INVASION FROM THE EAST

Eastern Europe was part of the Byzantine empire, which was the Roman empire in the east. At its heart was the magnificent city of Constantinople, where the emperor lived and ruled. At its peak, the empire had stretched from Armenia in the east, throughout Asia Minor, across the sea of Marmora and through the Balkans as far as the river Danube. During the course of its history the Byzantine empire had fought many times against invaders from the east. In the middle of the 11th century it was struggling against the Seljuk Turks. In 1071, at the battle of Manzikert, the Seljuks defeated the Byzantine emperor and took over the area of Anatolia (the Asian part of Turkey). This was a major catastrophe as Anatolia was the area where the emperor recruited his soldiers. Alexius Comnenus became emperor in 1081 and was determined to restore the empire.

THE BYZANTINE STRUGGLE WITH THE NORMANS

The Byzantine empire was also having to struggle in another direction at this time. Southern Italy had been part of the empire, but it had been conquered by the Normans under Robert Guiscard. Guiscard's intention was to march on Constantinople and, to this end, he attacked Greece in 1081. Alexius Comnenus enlisted the help of the Venetian fleet and managed to slow down the advance of the Normans. In 1085 Robert Guiscard died suddenly and his sons quarrelled among themselves. As we have seen, the pope had been encouraging the Norman advance in southern Italy in his struggle against the German emperor. The Byzantine struggle against the Normans could therefore also be seen as a struggle against the pope.

THE STRUGGLE BETWEEN THE EASTERN AND WESTERN CHURCHES

The Byzantine empire was Christian but it did not acknowledge the pope in Rome as the head of the church. The churches in the east and west had developed separately in the 4th and 5th centuries when the western Roman empire was being invaded by barbarian tribes. The language used in the eastern church was Greek and it became known as the Greek Orthodox church. In 1054 the Latin and the Greek Christian churches separated over doctrinal matters. Both thought that they were the true Christian church and that their leaders had the right to be the leader of Christendom. The death of Robert Guiscard made relationships between the pope and the Byzantine emperor easier. In 1089 Urban II lifted the excommunication that had been put on the emperor by his predecessor and the two churches began cautiously to negotiate with each other. Although relations between Alexius Comnenus and Urban II were friendly, there was, nevertheless, an underlying struggle for supremacy.

STRUGGLES IN THE ISLAMIC WORLD

Other struggles were going on within the empire of Islam. As with the Christian world, the Muslims were not united. The southern part of Spain was ruled by the Umayyad dynasty and the Christian kings of northern Spain, supported by the pope, were engaged in a war against them to try to push them out of the country. In the near east, in the late 11th century, there were two dynasties struggling to be acknowledged as the leaders of Islam – the Abbasids and the Fatimids. The Abbasid caliph ruled from Baghdad and the Fatimid caliph from Cairo. The caliph, the successor to the prophet Mohammed, was both a religious and a secular ruler. Support for the different caliphates came from the two main branches of Islam – the Sunni and the Shia. The Sunnites supported the Abbasids, the Shi'ites supported the Fatimids.

By the middle of the 11th century the Abbasids had become more or less rulers in name only because in 1055 the Seljuk Turks had attacked Baghdad. They were Sunni Muslims and their leader had taken over the running of the Abbasid empire, giving himself the title of sultan ('he with authority'). In 1071 the Seljuks took Jerusalem from the Fatimids. In 1092 the empire was divided into five large territories. The major cities of the empire became autonomous (self-ruling) emirates governed by atabegs, who began to make war on each other.

LIVING CONDITIONS IN THE EAST

Unlike the west, the near east was highly cultivated, fruitful and wealthy. The caliphs ruled from capital cities with the help of many officials. Luxury goods were exported all over the world; the textile industry flourished; mathematics, science, medicine and education were highly advanced. The Muslim conquerors left the local inhabitants to till the fields and tolerated their religions in return for taxes. Jerusalem was a holy city for both Muslims and Christians. Muslim control did not necessarily mean persecution for the Christians living there but, after the takeover of Anatolia by the Seljuks, it became more difficult and dangerous for pilgrims to travel overland from Europe to Jerusalem. Alexius Comnenus, looking for an opportunity to regain his empire, saw that the Seljuk Turks were weak because of internal disputes and aggression. He lacked soldiers, however. The west had soldiers aplenty so in 1095 he appealed to the pope, as a leader of influence in the west, to come to his aid.

On your A4 map, on which you marked the situation in Europe, the area under the control of the Muslims is shaded. **?**
1. Mark the caliphates of the Abbasids, Fatimids and Umayyads.
2. Find a way of showing on the map the struggles going on between the various rulers and nations, possibly by inventing symbols for them and then linking them with lines and arrows to show the direction of the struggles.

Sunni and Shi'ite Muslims

The divisions in the two major branches of the Muslim faith reflected different beliefs about the caliphs, who had followed the prophet Mohammed. The Sunnites believed that the first three caliphs after Mohammed were the true ones, but the Shi'ites believed that only the fourth, Ali, was a true caliph because he was married to the Prophet's daughter, Fatima. In their view, only the descendants of Fatima had the right to be caliphs.

Organising your information

It is most important that you present any background information in a way that you can easily understand and refer to, because you probably will not have studied this part of the world at this period before. You could start a card index system (or even a computer database) listing words, concepts, personalities or places that are new to you, with brief details. A card index system is very useful for revision, too.

THE KEY ISSUE

- What caused the first crusade?

THE KEY SKILLS

Analysis

Explanation

Assessment

Peter the Hermit

Peter came from Amiens in France. He had once been a monk but had become a wandering preacher. He was a short, ugly man, who walked barefoot or rode a donkey; he was said to resemble his donkey in looks. He wore ragged woollen clothes and lived on a diet of wine and fish. According to legend, he had tried to make a pilgrimage to Jerusalem but had not managed to reach it because of Turkish opposition. His preaching had a dramatic effect on his listeners. He was regarded as a holy man: people even pulled hairs from his donkey's tail to keep as holy relics.

Pope Urban's Appeal

THE BYZANTINE EMPEROR

In 1095 circumstances seemed to be favourable for Alexius Comnenus to start to win back his empire. He was a very able general, the Muslim forces were involved with internal disputes and his Norman enemy, Robert Guiscard, had died, leaving his relatives arguing about their inheritance. What he needed, however, was soldiers, especially as Anatolia, the recruiting ground of the Byzantine empire, was under Muslim control. He appealed to his brother in Christ, Pope Urban II, to send knights from the west. He wanted military help but he appealed to the pope on religious grounds. Knowing that Jerusalem was a very important place to all Christians and that pilgrimage was an important aspect of living the holy life and gaining salvation, he stressed the fact that Jerusalem was under the control of infidels, that the Holy City was being desecrated and that pilgrims were being persecuted and harassed. He appealed to Christian to go to the aid of Christian.

THE POPE

It is possible that a previous pope, Gregory VII, may have had plans to send or lead a force to the east to help the Byzantines and that Urban thought that the time was right to follow this up. He may have thought that if he could mobilise a large Christian force to go to the rescue of the Byzantine empire then he would prove that he was the stronger leader and ought to be acknowledged as the overall leader of Christendom. Urban may have sent letters to France, but he certainly travelled to Clermont for a council and there made an appeal on Alexius' behalf for knights to go to the aid of Jerusalem and Christians in the east. We have accounts of Urban's speech written by people who claimed to be present at the time, but they did not write their accounts until after the success of the first crusade, so they may have been influenced by this. We do know that the sermon was extremely effective. It lit a flame of enthusiasm and support in the western world, and led to thousands of people stitching a cloth cross to their shoulders and making their way across Europe, through unimaginable hardships, to go to the rescue of the Holy Land.

Peter the Hermit at the head of the first wave of crusaders

Infidel – someone of a religion other than Christianity

THE POOR

After the council at Clermont, other preachers took up the message and spread it to all kinds and classes of people in northern France. One of these preachers was Peter the Hermit. It is thought that the pope intended to limit the call to the knights but he had little control over these popular preachers, whose preaching we know little about except that it was extremely effective. Harvests had been poor in northern France in that year, so perhaps many thought that they had little to lose and everything to gain by going to the Holy City of Jerusalem. Thousands of peasants sold what little they had and followed Peter.

JERUSALEM

Urban's speech stressed the importance to Christians of Jerusalem. In one account, by Robert of Rheims, the pope calls it the 'navel of the world', the very place of connection between God and man, as the umbilical cord connects the child to the mother. In all medieval maps Jerusalem is shown as being in the physical centre of the world. The same account goes on, 'this royal city, placed at the centre of the world, is now held captive by her enemies and is enslaved to pagan rites by a people which does not acknowledge God. So she asks and prays to be liberated and calls on you unceasingly to come to her aid.' Jerusalem is personified here as pleading with the western Christians.

It was a place of pilgrimage, where the Christian could go to do penance for his or her sins. Urban promised that responding to the call to rescue Jerusalem would be effective as a penance for sin. The exact nature of the mission was not clear but it was regarded as some sort of pilgrimage in arms, and the vows taken were those of pilgrims. There may also have been some idea of taking vengeance on those who had despoiled Christ's own special place and his people, the Christian brothers of the westerners.

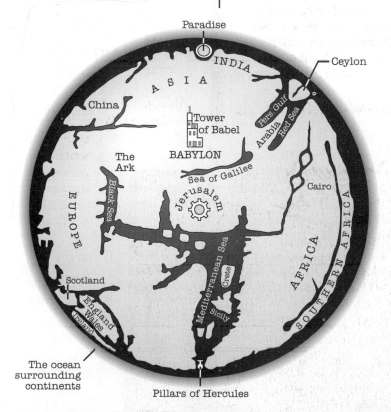

This map, taken from one made by monks in the 13th century, shows Jerusalem at the centre of the world

THE KEY ISSUE

● What were the motives of the first crusaders?

THE KEY SKILLS

Analysis

Explanation

Interpretation

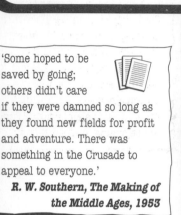

'Some hoped to be saved by going; others didn't care if they were damned so long as they found new fields for profit and adventure. There was something in the Crusade to appeal to everyone.'

R. W. Southern, *The Making of the Middle Ages*, 1953

The Response of the Knights

TOO MANY KNIGHTS, TOO MUCH FIGHTING

Urban was from a northern French noble family. He would have known the ways and needs of knights very well, especially in an area where there were problems because of a shortage of land and squabbles over inheritance. He said, according to Robert of Rheims, 'This land which you inhabit, shut in on all sides by the seas and surrounded by mountain peaks, is too narrow for your large population, nor does it abound in wealth, and it furnishes scarcely food enough for its cultivators. Hence it is that you murder and devour each other, that you wage war and that very many among you perish … let therefore hatred depart from among you, let your quarrels end, let wars cease, and let all dissensions and controversies slumber.' The pope had encouraged them to go and fight the infidel in Spain: now he was giving them another purpose – to fight for Christ in the Holy Land. Fulcher of Chartres records Urban as saying, 'Let those who have been accustomed to make private war against the faithful carry on a successful war against infidels … Let those who for a long time have been robbers now become soldiers of Christ. Let those who once fought against brothers and relatives now fight against barbarians.' Christian knights going off to fight in the east would ease the turbulence in the west.

THE KNIGHT'S DILEMMA

Knights had a problem in that their whole reason for being was to fight and to kill, and yet they were Christians and to kill was a sin. If they died in battle they died with their sins unforgiven. In France Christian knight was fighting Christian knight. As far as we know they were extremely concerned about the salvation of their souls, and yet there was not really a part for them to play in the church. Robert of Rheims records Urban as telling them to 'take this road for the remission of your sins, assured of the unfailing glory of the kingdom of heaven'. He appears to be promising them forgiveness of their sins if they took part in this particular war. This would solve the knight's problem. He would be able to fulfil his calling as a soldier and save his soul at the same time.

When you have read this chapter, draw up a list of the causes of the crusades. Historians do not agree on the order of importance of these causes and it is sometimes difficult to remember who holds which views.

Here is a method of analysis that may help you: make a table, like the one below, putting your list of causes in the first column and writing in the names of the historians whose works you have at the head of the other columns. Read the relevant chapters in the texts that you have. When you find that an historian writes about one of these causes, put a tick in the appropriate column. Add page numbers for future reference. In some cases all your historians will mention the same point but, in others, only one or two will make it. You will soon begin to see how historians have different interpretations.

?

Cause of crusade	Author 1	Author 2	Author 3	Author 4
Pope wanted control of Christendom				
Knights wanted land				

THE LURE OF WEALTH

Those in the west knew that luxury goods came from the east. The Holy Land is described in the Bible as a 'land flowing with milk and honey'. Some knights would have taken up the cross because they could see that they had a better chance of establishing themselves and gaining property in the Holy Land. Certainly one knight, Baldwin of Boulogne, who eventually became King of Jerusalem, took his wife and small children with him, which would indicate that he intended to stay in the east. Some of the peasants who responded to the call may well have felt that they had little in the way of this world's goods to lose and everything to gain by going to the Holy Land.

THE CHIVALROUS IDEAL

One of the entertainments for knights in Europe was to listen to poems, called *chansons de geste*, which narrated legends of the exploits of famous knights, especially in the time of Charlemagne, the first Holy Roman emperor. *The Song of Roland*, for example, was composed towards the end of the 11th century and tells of betrayal, of revenge and of slaughtering the infidel. It expresses the knightly ideal of the duty to protect family, lands and religion by attacking and killing the enemy. Urban's speech may therefore also have appealed to the knight's sense of honour and duty to protect the Christian religion.

THE IMPORTANCE OF RELIGION

Some of the crusaders may have been motivated by social and economic factors, others by political factors, but historians agree that religious factors were common to all. When Urban spoke of the campaign he appeared to liken it to a pilgrimage. He granted, to those who took up the call, the privileges of pilgrims – he protected their property while they were away, and they did not have to pay their debts until they came back. These people were moving out in faith to unknown territory – few can have envisaged the hardships that were to follow. Perhaps they were angry that Christ's inheritance had been destroyed, that pilgrims were prevented from reaching their goal. Perhaps they confused the earthly city of Jerusalem with the new heavenly Jerusalem that the Bible says is to come at the end of time. But we do know that it was important for them to have their sins forgiven and to make sure that, even if they had little in this world, they were going to get what Christ had promised them in the next. They were going to Jerusalem.

This 13th-century drawing shows a crusader knight kneeling to pay homage

The motives of the crusaders

It is difficult at this distance, and with very few sources to help us, to judge the motives of the first crusaders. One way we can infer them is by what the knights did afterwards. Of those who survived, most returned home after fulfilling their pilgrim vows in Jerusalem. Some stayed in the east, however, and established their own lands there. During the course of the first crusade it was the rank and file who continually urged the leaders to go on to Jerusalem, which, from the beginning, was their goal.

THE KEY ISSUE

● What happened on the first crusade?

THE KEY SKILLS

Analysis
Recording

The leaders of the first crusade (1)

Northern France and the Rhineland

Hugh of Vermandois – brother of the French king. He met Urban II in Italy and was given the papal banner. He was caught in a storm and came ashore in Byzantine territory, where he was arrested and taken to Constantinople. He was treated well but reports of his ill-treatment affected the crusading troops.

Robert, count of Flanders – powerful Flanders was the richest area in northern Europe.

Stephen, count of Blois – a powerful nobleman married to Adela, daughter of William the Conqueror.

Robert, duke of Normandy – the son of William the Conqueror

Eustace of Boulogne – elder brother of Godfrey de Bouillon and Baldwin of Boulogne.

Godfrey de Bouillon, duke of Lower Lorraine – he had fought against Urban on the side of the emperor, Henry IV. He therefore felt he had to make atonement for this. He mortgaged his possessions to go.

Baldwin of Boulogne – the youngest of the three brothers, who had originally been intended for the church. He sold what land he had and took his wife and family with him to the east.

The Journey Begins

THE RESPONSE TO URBAN'S APPEAL

Alexius Comnenus had asked Urban II for knights from the west. Urban appointed Adhémar, bishop of Le Puy, to be his representative on the campaign and he urged the knights to make their way to Constantinople. Nobody could have anticipated that, before the knights were ready, thousands of other men, women and children would also respond to the call. Inspired by popular preachers, they sold all that they had to walk across Europe with whatever weapons they could muster in order to rescue the Holy City from the infidel. Peter the Hermit was one of the leaders of this first wave, which is sometimes called the People's Crusade. Walter Sansavoir, a knight from Poissy, was another and so was Emich, count of Leisingen.

THE MASSACRE OF THE JEWS

Many of the crusaders were poor. They did not have money or supplies for the journey and they had to live off the land that they passed through. As there were so many of them, pillage and plunder were common. When they reached Germany, someone, possibly Emich, pointed out that Christ's enemies were nearer at hand than Jerusalem: he was referring to the Jews who inhabited many of the cities in Germany and flourished as money-lenders. In Metz, Meinz and Cologne the Jewish communities were attacked and men, women and children massacred. The Jews offered money to the crusaders in return for their lives, and some fled to the bishop's palace for protection, but even there they were not safe. They were slaughtered mercilessly.

THE FIRST WAVE IN ASIA MINOR

Peter the Hermit and his followers reached Constantinople on 1 August 1096. Alexius was concerned about having masses of poor people within Constantinople so he made arrangements for them to be ferried quickly across the Bosphorus into Asia Minor. He advised them to wait there until the main force of knights arrived. The crusaders set up a base at Cibotos and, again being short of food, they plundered the nearby villages and massacred the inhabitants. They thought that they were killing the infidel and did not realise that many of them were Greek Christians. The various European nationalities within the group also fought and quarrelled amongst themselves. In the autumn of 1096 a Turkish force broke into the camp and massacred most of them. Alexius Comnenus sent a relief force and managed to rescue some who were holding out in a ruined castle, but this first wave was virtually wiped out. The easy victory for the Turks left them thinking that was little to fear from the European forces.

THE KNIGHTS GATHER

Meanwhile the knights had been preparing, and they set out for Constantinople. They came from four main areas and formed distinct groups throughout the campaign. There was no overall leader and many knights were serving the richer knights in order to make sure that they had supplies. There were changes of loyalty during the campaign. We do not know precisely the motives of the leaders but they certainly included men of immense ambition. From northern France came Hugh of Vermandois, brother of the French king; Robert, count of Flanders; Stephen, count of Blois, whose letters to his wife form an important source; and Robert, duke of Normandy, who had mortgaged Normandy in order to get the money for his journey. Another group from northern France and the Rhineland comprised three brothers: Eustace of Boulogne, Godfrey de Bouillon and Baldwin of Boulogne. From southern France came Raymond de Saint Gilles, count of Toulouse, and Adhémar, bishop of Le Puy. The Normans of southern Italy, former enemies of Byzantium, were represented by Bohemond of Taranto, son of Robert Guiscard, and his nephew Tancred.

PERSONAL RIVALRIES

The knights began to arrive in Constantinople in the winter of 1096 and were all assembled by the spring of 1097. Alexius was concerned that he could not entirely trust these knights to carry out his purposes, especially as his enemy, Bohemond, was one of the leaders. He therefore demanded that they swear an oath of loyalty to him when they reached Constantinople. The swearing of oaths was not common in the Byzantine empire but it was part and parcel of the feudal way of life in the west and would have been treated very seriously by the knights. Some were very reluctant to take the oath and Tancred avoided it altogether by slipping away across the Bosphorus by night. Raymond de Saint Gilles appears to have objected on religious grounds and so Alexius modified the oath for him. It is thought that Alexius favoured Raymond as the leader of the expedition because he could see that there was rivalry between him and Bohemond.

Alexius now had his fighting force. It was not what he expected. Perhaps he was not what they had expected. Alexius made no attempt to take personal command of the expedition but he gave them supplies and military advisers and shipped them across the Bosphorus so that they could start their journey to Jerusalem.

The leaders of the first crusade (2)

The southern French

Raymond de Saint Gilles, count of Toulouse – aged about 60, he probably hoped to be the secular leader. He had fought in Spain against the Muslims.

Adhémar, bishop of Le Puy – the man that the pope wanted to be the leader. He was highly respected for his piety but not forceful enough to exert overall authority.

The Normans of southern Italy

Bohemond of Taranto – the son of Robert Guiscard. Robert had died in 1085 and left most of his estates to the son of his second marriage. Bohemond therefore had little land. The Byzantines thought that he was using the crusade as a cloak for his own purposes. He was the military genius of the campaign.

Tancred – nephew of Bohemond, only about 17 years old and in the retinue of Bohemond. He too was a great military leader.

Plunder – the spoils of war, the treasure or goods of the enemy. It was customary for medieval knights to treat plunder as payment for their services and they used it to finance their wars.

At this stage it is important to know *what* happened rather than *why* it happened. You will need to read accounts of the first crusade in your texts. Make a timeline to show the main events. Many texts have a chronology, which will help you.

THE KEY ISSUE

● Why was the first crusade successful?

THE KEY SKILLS

Analysis

Assessment

Explanation

Recording

Evaluation

Siege tower – a wooden tower that could be pushed close to a wall so that soldiers could climb up and scale the wall with some protection from the assault of the enemy

You will need to read more detailed accounts than this to understand the story fully. Now might be a good opportunity to watch the BBC film on the first crusade, if you have it. (See page 13.)

Extend the timeline that you started to make in chapter 2 and annotate it with details of the battles. Make a note of why the crusaders were successful at each stage and how their relationships with each other and the Byzantine empire changed. Also make a note of the effect of the supernatural on the crusaders.

Try to group the reasons for their success under such factors as: disunity of the Muslim opposition, military tactics, aid from the Byzantine emperor, and supernatural elements.

Then answer the question: *Why was the first crusade successful?*

Towards Jerusalem

NICAEA

The first stage in the campaign of the knights was to capture the city of Nicaea, which was a town defended by strong ramparts and a lake. The crusaders had hoped to take the city by storm but they had to besiege it. The siege lasted for a month, until Alexius sent ships to blockade the lake. Alexius arranged for the city to be surrendered to himself, which meant that the crusaders were denied the plunder that they had hoped for; this caused resentment against the emperor. Alexius agreed that he would reward the crusaders with money and supplies, provided that they all took the oath of loyalty to him. Tancred then took the oath. Alexius sent Tatikios, a Greek officer, with the army to advise on military tactics and to act as a guide.

DORYLAEUM AND EDESSA

On 1 July 1097 the first open battle between crusaders and the Turks took place at Dorylaeum. The crusaders divided the army into two divisions. They sent Raymond's force ahead and held Bohemond's back. The Turks attacked but they didn't realise that they were only attacking half of the crusading army. When the first division was about to break, the rest of the army came up. The Turks panicked and Bohemond launched the charge of the knights. The leader of the Turks, the sultan of Rum, escaped but his treasure chest was captured. He took his revenge by smashing the water cisterns in the country through which the crusaders had to pass, exposing them and their horses to raging thirst in the fierce Anatolian sun.

The crusaders continued to cross Asia Minor. The main body swung north but Baldwin of Boulogne left the main force and crossed to Cilicia. Here he helped the Armenian ruler of Edessa to defeat a Turkish attack and was rewarded by being adopted by him. Shortly afterwards, the ruler of Edessa was killed and Baldwin proclaimed himself as count in March 1098. Edessa therefore became the first of the Frankish states in the east.

ANTIOCH

For the main force the next problem was the city of Antioch, which had, 100 years previously, belonged to the Byzantine emperor. It had vast walls climbing a mountain, with a citadel at the crest. The crusaders besieged the city. Alexius sent supplies to the Christian army but there was never enough food. From January 1098 men began to desert. In February the Greek general, Tatikios, left and his departure caused more resentment against the Byzantine empire. By about the end of May, they heard that a great Turkish army was on the way. Bohemond wanted control of Antioch. He found a captain in one of the towers who was ready to betray the city to the crusaders and let Bohemond's force in by night. The crusading army took control of the city, but soon they in turn were besieged by the relieving Turkish army. The crusaders were starving in the city. They knew that they had to go out and fight but there was little hope of success. Then one of the peasants with Raymond, Peter Bartholomew, had a vision of the lance which had pierced the side of Christ. He went on to find this in the cathedral. Some doubted the authenticity of the lance but the majority saw it as a miracle and a sign that God was with them. The army fasted for three days, marched barefoot round the churches and confessed their sins. On 28 June they marched out of Antioch carrying the lance. The Turkish army fled. The crusaders had followed the sign and God had given them success.

DIVISIONS AND DISSENSIONS

After this, they were reluctant to move on. There were arguments amongst the leaders as to who possessed Antioch. It should have gone to Alexius. Hugh of Vermandois asked him to come and take possession. He found that Alexius had been on his way to relieve Antioch but had turned back when he met Stephen of Blois, who was returning to Europe. It looked as though Alexius had betrayed the crusaders. Adhémar died in July 1098. Bohemond argued that he should be lord of Antioch and he was opposed by Raymond of Toulouse. This argument lasted until 1099 when Raymond's own men forced him to begin the advance on Jerusalem. Others followed, except Bohemond.

JERUSALEM

Jerusalem was a well-fortified city, rocky and difficult to attack. Supplies came in by sea to the port of Jaffa at this time and so the crusaders were able to build siege towers. Once more it was an element of the supernatural that raised morale and gave them the incentive to go forward. One of the priests had a vision of the ghost of Adhémar, who told them to fast, pray and march barefoot round Jerusalem. This they did. The siege towers enabled them to gain footholds, they broke in and opened the gates to their comrades. There then began a terrible massacre of all the inhabitants of Jerusalem. They had achieved their goal. They had started with forces of about 40 000 and these had been reduced to about 12 000. Against all the odds they had succeeded. To them this could only mean that God had set his seal of approval on their enterprise.

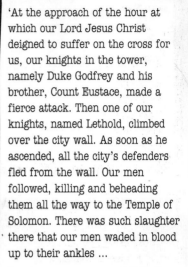

The capture of Jerusalem

'At the approach of the hour at which our Lord Jesus Christ deigned to suffer on the cross for us, our knights in the tower, namely Duke Godfrey and his brother, Count Eustace, made a fierce attack. Then one of our knights, named Lethold, climbed over the city wall. As soon as he ascended, all the city's defenders fled from the wall. Our men followed, killing and beheading them all the way to the Temple of Solomon. There was such slaughter there that our men waded in blood up to their ankles ...

Soon our men were running all around the city, seizing gold and silver, horses and mules, and houses filled with all kinds of goods.

Rejoicing and weeping for joy, our people came to the sepulchre of Jesus our Saviour to worship and pay their debt. At dawn our men cautiously went up to the roof of the Temple and attacked the Saracen men and women, beheading them with naked swords ...

No one ever saw or heard of such slaughter of pagan peoples, for funeral pyres were formed of them like pyramids and no one knows their numbers save God alone.'

From Gesta Francorum et aliorum Hierosolymitanorum

THE KEY ISSUES

- How were the crusader states organised and governed?
- How did the crusader states function economically?
- What difference did Latin rule make to the Holy Land?

THE KEY SKILLS

Analysis
Assessment
Recording

1. From a modern atlas, find out more about the land of the Latin states, for example the physical features of mountains, deserts and rivers, the annual rainfall, the average temperatures and so on. Mark these on a map. Then do the same exercise looking at a map of northern Europe, especially France. By noting the similarities and differences, make a list of the problems you think that the crusaders would have encountered in settling in the east and in trying to preserve their western way of life.

2. Make a diagram to show the social structure of Outremer, including all the different peoples.

The Founding of the Crusader States

OUTREMER

When Baldwin of Boulogne was proclaimed count of Edessa in 1098 the first Crusader, or Latin, state in the east was born. The second was created when Bohemond became prince of Antioch. After the capture of Jerusalem in 1099 the crusaders agreed that the city should be kept and defended. The clergy thought that a theocracy should be established as it was inappropriate for a king to rule in the place where Jesus, the King of Kings, had been crucified. The lords who had fought their way to Jerusalem thought differently, however, and quickly chose Godfrey de Bouillon as their leader.

Godfrey took the title of Defender of the Holy Sepulchre but when he died in 1100 his brother, Baldwin of Boulogne, took the title of King of Jerusalem. Initially there was little land for him to rule over and most of the crusaders, having done what they set out to do, went home. However, in the next 30 years Baldwin I and his successor, Baldwin II, made the kingdom of Jerusalem into a large and coherent territory. A fourth state was added in 1109 when Bertrand de Saint Gilles (son of Raymond) took the city of Tripoli and became the count. These states were known in the west as Outremer, which is French for 'beyond the sea'.

THE CHURCH

The church in Outremer came under the control of the pope in Rome, and the language used in the churches was Latin. The main religious centre was Jerusalem, where the great festivals of the church were celebrated. At the head of the ecclesiastical organisation were the patriarchs of Jerusalem and Antioch. The most important church was the church of the Holy Sepulchre in Jerusalem, which owned extensive estates both in Europe and the Holy Land. Tithes were paid by the lords of lands, rather than by individual tenants which was the case in Europe, into a central office at the cathedral; they were then redistributed to the various parishes. There were frequent disputes about tithes.

GOVERNMENT AND STRUCTURE

The ideas that the crusaders adopted about how society should be governed were, at first, naturally those that they had brought with them, especially the western idea of feudalism. The king was at the head of society, and he gave fiefs to his vassals, the knights, who gave him military service in return. The king controlled justice, warfare and the collection of taxes. By contrast with Europe, where fiefs were in land, fiefs in the Holy Land were frequently in money as the majority of the settlers lived in the towns.

In order to control the countryside and defend the kingdom, many castles were built for military reasons and small settlements grew up around them. These were often inhabited by burgesses, free Franks of a lower social order than the knights, who were the footsoldiers or sergeants in time of war. They had their own law courts, which used trial by ordeal as in Europe. Cases where a burgess had a disagreement with a knight were dealt with at the *haute court*, or king's court.

THE NATIVE POPULATION: MUSLIMS

Most mosques were converted to Christian churches and public worship according to the Islamic faith (except in Acre and, perhaps, Jerusalem) was banned. However, the Franks appear to have made no attempt to convert the native Muslim people to Christianity. They could not have survived economically without the native workers of the land and the tolls charged to allow Muslim traders to cross the country to the coast. The Franks tended to live close to each other in the towns, and left the day-to-day overseeing of their land to the local people, who were forced to pay taxes rather than to render services, as they would have done in western Europe.

Many of the Muslim methods of administration were retained. The local Muslim official settled disputes in the villages and administered justice but higher judicial affairs were dealt with by the Franks. Perhaps the Muslims expected the Franks either to move on or to be assimilated into the ways of the country before long, as previous invaders had been, but this was not to be the case. Some Muslims, probably from the higher ranks, emigrated to Damascus, where they constantly urged the ruler to launch a counter crusade against the Franks.

THE NATIVE POPULATION: CHRISTIANS

Most of the native population consisted of Christian Syrians, who were themselves divided into several religious groups. They were craftsmen and farmers who had been tolerated when the land had been ruled by the Arabs and the Turks. They welcomed the Franks at first but found that their lives changed very little with the Latin Christians in charge. There were also Armenian and Greek Christians living mainly in the coastal towns, especially within the principality of Antioch. Each of the Christian communities obeyed its own clergy.

The Franks regarded the Latin church as being superior and were very inflexible. Relationships with the Byzantine empire were further soured by the attitude of the Latin Christians to the Greek Orthodox Christians. The eastern Christians found that life under the Franks was less tolerable than life under the Muslims, when at least they had had some kind of autonomy. For this reason the eastern Christians, who could and perhaps should have been valued allies of the Franks, felt no sense of loyalty and, after three generations of Latin rule, began to ally themselves with the Muslim leaders.

Theocracy – a state run by the church
Patriarch – the chief bishop of the church
Tithe – a tax of one tenth, usually of farm produce, paid to the church
Fief – the amount of land held by a knight in return for his services
Trial by ordeal – a way of putting a case to God for Him to decide whether the accused was innocent or guilty by performing a miracle. For example, the accused was instructed to pick up a red hot iron bar from a fire and carry it for so many paces. If after three days the burns were healing, the accused was innocent; if they were not healing, the accused was guilty.

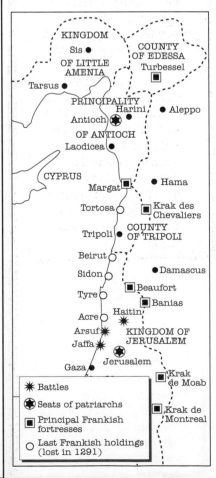

The Latin states at their peak

THE KEY ISSUES

- How did the relationships between Outremer and the west affect the development of the crusader states?
- What role did the Italian cities play in the life of Outremer?
- What sort of society developed in the Latin states?

THE KEY SKILLS

Analysis

Assessment

Interpretation

Explanation

Recording

1. The story of the kings and queens of Jerusalem, their relationships to each other and the part they played in the development of Outremer is a very interesting and human story. It is also very complicated, as it is usually interwoven with the other events. In order to try to clarify this in your mind, and to have something to refer to later, make a copy of the family tree on this page. In your texts research the lives of the kings and queens and annotate the family tree with details of relationships to the east or the west, problems and factions, main events in their reign and so on.

2. Make a list of the areas in which the king of Jerusalem was likely to have problems.

3. Continue the list of similarities and differences between the lives of the Franks in the east and the west.

The Influence of the West

EAST AND WEST

The number of Latins living in the crusader states was never large. Sir Stephen Runciman estimates that there could only have been from two to three thousand adult members of the Frankish upper classes. This meant that they had to depend on the people around them in many ways, especially for economic survival. They could not avoid contact with the other occupants of the Holy Land and they had to change some of their habits in order to cope with the climate and the type of food that was available. They became accustomed, for instance, to bathing frequently and using perfume, something which to westerners was extremely effeminate.

They did, however, also have to rely on the west for provisions and for military aid. The west must have regarded the crusader states as partly their responsibility, as there was a sense that the success of the first crusade proved that it was God's will that the Holy Land should belong to the Franks. Every year, especially at Easter, pilgrims would arrive in Outremer, some of them anxious to kill the infidel for Christ, and in times of crisis other crusades were preached and forces sent to the aid of the king of Jerusalem.

THE ITALIAN CITIES

The crusader states depended heavily on support from the Italian maritime cities of Genoa, Pisa and Venice, which were trading cities anxious to expand their interests in the east. They entered into agreements with the king of Jerusalem to bring supplies and troops to Outremer in return for tax exemptions and other legal immunities. As a result, they formed colonies within the cities, especially the coastal ports. Their loyalties were to their own cities and the king of Jerusalem had to pay a price for their aid. Much of the profit earned by trade in the coastal towns went into Italian coffers.

Defence was always a problem. The crusader states occupied a narrow coastal strip and they were in danger of attacks from all sides, especially from the Egyptians who had a considerable fleet. They had no sea power, apart from that which had to be bought from the Italians, and they had only a small force of fighting men to call on.

NEGOTIATING WITH THE ENEMY

The Franks who lived in Outremer, however, did know the countryside and the way of life. They negotiated treaties with their neighbours, as they knew that they did not have the manpower to fight continuously on all fronts. Some sort of compromise with the Muslims was essential, but pilgrims and knights who came from the west did not view things in the same light. Some were horrified at what they perceived to be the effeminate life of luxury lived by the Frankish inhabitants. They considered that any compromise with the infidel was unacceptable and often could not tell a Syrian Christian from a Muslim. Frequently, those that were the least tolerant were the most powerful leaders who expected to have a say in the conduct of military campaigns. This led to quarrels among leaders and weakened the authority of the king of Jerusalem, especially in times of war. The problem came to a head in the second crusade, as we shall see in chapter 7.

THE CROWN

The opposing ideals and interests of those from the east and the west can also be seen in the gradual weakening of the authority of the king and the quarrels over the succession. When the first nobles in the east died, their children and newcomers from the west took over their lands. In 1131 Baldwin II died and was succeeded by his daughter Melisende. Baldwin had anticipated that problems might arise because he had no male heir and so he had arranged for Melisende to marry Fulk of Anjou, who ruled as king. Fulk clashed with nobles from the east and the conflicts that followed undermined the power of the monarchy.

Between about 1130 and 1160 the richest of the nobles developed into a tight knit group. Power was concentrated in the ten or so families who owned the top 24 lordships. In the reign of Baldwin IV (1174–1185), who suffered from leprosy, various factions grew up supporting different contenders for the throne. This weakened the kingdom at the very time when the Muslims were becoming united. Baldwin IV was succeeded by his nephew, Baldwin V, but he was only a child. There were quarrels over the regency between the eastern lords, who supported Raymond of Tripoli, and the western, who supported Guy of Lusignan. After only a few months, Baldwin V died and Guy had himself crowned king. Raymond went to Tiberias and there considered entering into a treaty with Saladin, the Muslim leader. The western faction did not understand that truces were necessary so that forces could be conserved and built up. When another truce was broken and Tiberias was besieged by Saladin, King Guy was swayed by arguments from the western faction to commit his whole army to the rescue. This led to disaster for the Frankish armies at Hattin in 1187.

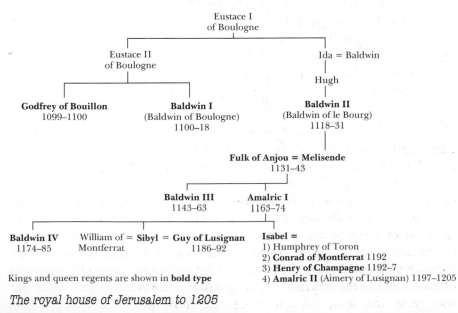

The royal house of Jerusalem to 1205

Kings and queen regents are shown in **bold type**

The Franks

'The Franks ... are an accursed race, the members of which do not assimilate except with their own kin.

Mysterious are the works of the Creator, the author of all things. When one comes to recount cases regarding the Franks, he cannot but glorify Allah (exalted is he!) and sanctify him, for he sees them as animals possessing the virtues of courage and fighting but nothing else; just as animals have only the virtues of strength and carrying loads.'

Usamah, a Muslim prince of Shaizar, born in 1095

The west becomes east

'We, who were westerners, find ourselves transformed into inhabitants of the east. The Italian or Frenchman of yesterday, transplanted here, has become a Galilean or Palestinian. A man from Rheims or Chartres has turned into a Syrian or a citizen of Antioch. We have already forgotten our native land ... Some men have already taken as wives Syrian or Armenian women, or even Saracens if they have been baptised ... one cultivates his vines, another his fields; they speak different tongues, and have already managed to understand each other ... races utterly unlike each other live together in trust.'

Fulcher of Chartres, writing about 1120

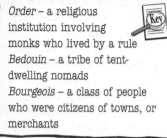

Order – a religious institution involving monks who lived by a rule
Bedouin – a tribe of tent-dwelling nomads
Bourgeois – a class of people who were citizens of towns, or merchants

Using the sources on this page and your texts, explain the military orders and their development. **?**

Knights and castles

Many of the famous castles, such as Krak des Chevaliers, belonged to the military orders. Here William of Tyre describes the way in which many of these castles, and other lands, were acquired:

'Humphrey of Toron, the king's constable, became weary of the continual responsibility and expense which devolved upon him in the care of the city of Banyas, his hereditary possession. Since he could not without aid suitably rule and protect it, with the king's consent he decided to share it equally with the brothers of the Hospital ... the brothers were to own one half of the city and all outlying dependencies, they were to pay one half of the expenses for all necessary and useful outlay, and to bear due responsibility for one half of the city.'

The Beginnings

THE CRUSADING IDEAL

There were two orders of fighting monks established in Outremer in the early years of its existence – the Knights of the Hospital of St John (the Hospitallers) and the Knights of the Temple (the Templars). This was something new, a way for the pious knight to find a way of saving his soul while at the same time following his calling. If there was a crusading ideal, it was the combination of the knight, fighting in the flesh against the infidel, with the monk, fighting in the spirit against the world, the flesh and the devil, and it was embodied in these military orders. They formed the only standing army that the kings of Jerusalem could call on. The orders became extremely rich and spread throughout Europe, their members frequently holding high office in European countries in later years.

THE HOSPITALLERS

When the crusaders besieged Jerusalem in 1099, there was in the city a small Christian hospital of St John the Almoner in the charge of a monk called Gerard. After the city had fallen into crusader hands, the hospital was enlarged and more monks were recruited. The monks also ran a hostel for pilgrims. Gerard began to organise the brotherhood on the lines of an independent religious order. From 1119 onwards it also began to protect pilgrims from attack and to include soldiers among its members. Godfrey de Bouillon granted Gerard, and this new order, a castle and two bakehouses in Jerusalem and it was not long before people in western Christendom were endowing it with properties in the west. Recruits flowed in because the order was semi-monastic and semi-military, which fulfilled a need for men whose only skills were military but who wanted to dedicate themselves to a religious life. The Hospitallers were recognised by the pope as a religious order in 1120.

THE TEMPLARS

The Knights Templar (the Poor Knights of Christ and the Temple of Solomon) were founded at about the same time by a Burgundian knight, Hugh of Payens. Their aim was to protect pilgrims from attacks by Muslims, or robbers, on their way to Jerusalem and the other holy places. At first there were only eight knights but the order soon grew to be immensely powerful and wealthy. The king granted them a house next to the royal palace, which had been the Temple of Solomon, and so they became known as the knights of the Temple. They were recruited from knights in the Holy Land and pilgrims coming to the Holy Land.

The Knights Templar dedicated themselves to the service of the poor, which in the Holy Land were chiefly pilgrims. Although the country was officially controlled by the Frankish armies after the capture of Jerusalem, there was still danger from Bedouin raids in the countryside of Judaea and Galilee. The almost permanent state of war also made the Muslim peasants much more hostile to the Christians than they had been before the crusades. The Knights Templar acted as guides and escorts and formed a kind of police force to patrol the pilgrim routes. The Templars were recognised as a religious order by the Pope in 1128.

THE STRUCTURE OF THE ORDERS

Both orders had the same structure. They were divided into three classes according to their social origins: the knights, the sergeants and the clergy. From the knights was chosen the Grand Master. He was necessarily of noble blood and ruled with autocratic powers. The sergeants were from less aristocratic, possibly bourgeois, families and the clergy acted as chaplains. The two orders came directly under the authority of the pope. They took a vow of poverty, chastity and obedience (the monastic vow) but they became a corps of extremely dedicated and able professional soldiers. From 1130 onwards members of the orders wore a uniform. This was unusual for soldiers and was inspired by monastic practice. The Templars wore a white tunic with a red cross and the Hospitallers wore a black tunic with a white cross.

The military orders were extremely valuable to the king of Jerusalem as a permanent, highly trained force with an extremely good knowledge of the country. They were known for their skill and courage, much feared by their enemies, and could be found fighting in the most difficult places. In 1128 Baldwin II had the idea of using the orders, with their élite troops, for his own purposes. However, their primary allegiance was to their own order, which was often a cause of tension.

A Knight Templar rides out to battle

The Templars

William of Tyre, who was born in the east around 1130, became the archbishop of Tyre and tutor to Baldwin IV. He wrote his memoirs, which cover the history of Jerusalem from 1127 to 1184, after he had retired to Rome in 1183. Here he describes the growth of the Templars:

'Although the Templars had been established for nine years there were as yet only nine in number. After this period ... they began to increase, and their possessions multiplied ... The Templars prospered so greatly that today there are in the order about three hundred knights who wear the white mantle and ... an almost countless number of lesser brothers ... They are said to have vast possessions, both on this side of the sea and beyond. There is not a province in the Christian world today which does not bestow some part of its possessions on this brethren and their property is reported to be equal to the riches of kings.'

St Bernard met Templars in Rome and France. This is what he wrote about them:

'They come and go at a sign from their commander; they wear the clothes which he gives them ... They are wary of all excess in food and clothing, desiring only what is needful ... No idlers or lookers-on are to be found in their company; when they are not on active service ... or eating bread or giving thanks to Heaven, they busy themselves with mending their clothes and their torn or tattered harness ... They crop their hair close because the Gospels tell them that it is a shame for a man to tend his hair. They are never seen combed and rarely washed, their beards are matted, they reek of dust and bear the stains of the heat and their harness.'

THE KEY ISSUES

- What part did the military orders play in Outremer?
- What was their relationship with the church?
- What was their relationship with the king of Jerusalem?

THE KEY SKILLS

Analysis
Assessment
Explanation
Evaluation

Assassins – a fanatical Shi'ite group which lived in the mountains of Syria. They murdered those who disagreed with them, and they took the drug hashish from which the name Assassin comes.

1. Make a list of the advantages and the disadvantages of the military orders to the kingdom and church of Jerusalem.

2. Consider the primary sources and their writers. Should we accept their verdict on the military orders at face value? How useful and reliable are these sources?

3. Answer the question: *How important were the military orders to the Latin states?*

The Development of the Orders

RELATIONS WITH THE CHURCH

The orders owed allegiance to the pope, not to the patriarch or to the king, but he was a long way away. Because they protected pilgrims the papacy rewarded them by giving them its protection, according them property rights over any booty they won from the Muslims and exempting them from paying any tithes on all territories taken from the infidel. However, they felt that their special position in the Holy Land entitled them to maintain their own interests above that of the Frankish church. They preferred to keep themselves to themselves and, over time, achieved a reputation for brutality and greed.

The church in Outremer must have resented the wealth and power of the orders; it certainly clashed with them over several matters. When the orders were entrusted with the defence of castles they promptly declared the castles ecclesiastical property and refused to pay tithes on them to the bishop. If anyone living on their land had been excommunicated they would receive him into their churches. William of Tyre accused them even of building such large buildings to the glory of their own order around the Church of the Holy Sepulchre that it became difficult to reach the church. They were also accused of ringing their bells so loudly that no one could hear the patriarch of Jerusalem when he preached. William also reported how the Hospitallers actually burst into the Church of the Holy Sepulchre on one occasion armed with bows and 'fired a great quantity of arrows'.

THE ORDERS AND THE KINGS OF JERUSALEM

Although valuable as a fighting force, the orders caused problems for the king of Jerusalem. At Ascalon in 1177, the Templars came to the rescue of the king and attacked and destroyed Saladin's forces. However, at Ascalon in 1153 the Knights Templar had insisted on entering the city themselves and would not allow others to follow them. This delayed the capture of the city for a month. In 1148 the Templars were blamed for the failure to take Damascus. At the battle of Hattin in 1187, the military orders fought and died with extreme courage but the hopeless situation in which the Frankish army found itself was caused by the fact that the Grand Master of the Templars had urged the king to go out to battle with the Muslims, rather than using traditional defensive tactics. At Arsuf in 1191, Richard I found them a mixed blessing. He was waiting to hold back the charge of the knights until the very last moment, when the Muslims would have been exhausted, but some of the Templars could not wait any longer and charged, the others following them. Richard was still able to save the situation but it was not the total success that he had wanted.

The orders had political as well as military influence on the king. In 1173 an alliance was proposed between the Franks and Rashid ed Din (leader of the Assassins and known as the Old Man of the Mountains) to oppose Saladin and Nureddin, powerful Muslim leaders. King Amalric agreed but the Templars were angry because one or two of the Assassin villages paid them protection money and they would lose this if they became allies. The Grand Master determined to wreck the agreement and murdered Rashid's envoys. Amalric was so angry he arrested the man responsible, even though the military orders were immune from arrest, and considered asking the pope to dissolve the order of the Templars. In the disputes about the succession following the death of Amalric in 1174, the candidate who had the support of the military orders also had the support of the west and was usually the stronger. The support of the orders was therefore of great importance.

The orders in peace

The wealth of the Templars described in the 12th century by Theodorich, a pilgrim to Jerusalem, who wrote an account of his visit as a guide for other pilgrims from the west: 'The Palace of Solomon ... abounds with rooms, solar chambers and buildings suitable for all manner of uses. Those who walk upon the roof find an abundance of gardens, courtyards, antechambers, vestibules and rainwater cisterns; while down below, it contains a wonderful number of baths, storehouses, granaries and magazines for the storage of wood and other needful provisions ... It is not easy for anyone to gain an idea of the power and wealth of the Templars for they and the Hospitallers have taken possession of almost all the cities and villages with which Judaea was once enriched, which were destroyed by the Romans, and have built castles everywhere, and filled them with garrisons, besides the very many, and, indeed, numberless estates, which they are well known to possess in other lands.'

John of Wurzburg, a pilgrim, writes in 1170 on the work of the Hospitallers: '... in various rooms is collected together an enormous multitude of sick people, both men and women, who are tended and restored to health daily at a very great expense. When I was there I learned that the whole number of these sick persons amounted to two thousand, of whom sometimes, in the course of one day and night, more than fifty are carried out dead, while many other fresh ones keep continually arriving. What more can I say? This same house supplies as many people outside it with victuals as it does those inside, in addition to the boundless charity which is daily bestowed on poor people, who beg their bread from door to door, so that the whole sum total of its expenses can surely never be calculated ...'

The Grand Master of the Templars

The orders in war

The siege of Damascus (1148), by the Wurzburg annalist: 'King Baldwin would have fulfilled his desire at Damascus, had not the greed, trickery and envy of the Templars got in his way. For they accepted a huge bribe from the Philistines [the enemy] to give secret aid to the besieged inhabitants. When they could not free the city by these means, they deserted the camp, the king and their companions, at night. Conrad III was enraged by this and, in hatred of the Templars' deceit, relinquished the siege and left the city saying that he would never again come to the aid of Jerusalem, neither himself nor any of his people. The king of Jerusalem, who also detested the arrogance of the Knights Templar, was deeply embarrassed and much grieved by this.'

The battle of Hattin (1187), by the author of the *Itinerarium regis Ricardi*:

'Then what a passionate rivalry of faith and courage ensued! Many of the captives, claiming to be Templars, vied together in a rush towards the butchers. Gladly they offered their necks to the swordsmen, under a holy pretence. Among these soldiers of Christ was a certain Templar called Nicholas. He was so successful in urging others to their death that, in the rush to get ahead, he himself only just managed to be the first to win the glorious martyrdom he so earnestly desired.'

William of Tyre describes how, at the siege of Ascalon (1153), part of the wall collapsed under the Christian bombardment:

'But Bernard de Tremble, the Master of the Templars, and his brethren had reached there much before the rest; he held the opening and allowed none but his own men to enter. It was charged that he kept the rest back in order that his own people, being the first to enter, might obtain the greater and richer of the spoils and plunder ...'

THE KEY ISSUE

What factors brought about Muslim recovery?

THE KEY SKILLS

Analysis

Interpretation

Recording

Danishmends – a Turkish dynasty inhabiting the north and centre of Anatolia

Vizier – a minister of state

Spellings

You will find different spellings of names and places in the books that you read. This is because the sources were written in different languages. Some translators use the English equivalent of certain names, while some leave them in the original language if it is a European one. The Muslim names were written in Arabic and so they have to be translated in some way that English readers will be able to understand and pronounce. Different translators do this in different ways. The name of Nureddin, for example, occurs also as Nur al Din and Nur ed Din: all are the same person.

1. Start to make a flow chart showing the stages of Muslim unity.
2. Take a copy of the map of Europe and the Near East from the back cover and shade it to show how the Muslim lands were united under Zengi and Nureddin.

Zengi and Nureddin

DIVISIONS

The first crusade was successful at a time when the Muslims were not only disunited in religious doctrine, but also warring against each other for reasons of politics and race. The Arabs, who had conquered the former Byzantine provinces of Syria, Palestine and Egypt, hated the Turks who had taken over their lands. The Turks themselves were split into rival clans. The Seljuk Turks fought against the Danishmends. The Turkish rulers of important cities such as Aleppo and Damascus were suspicious of each other and tried to prevent any one of them gaining more power than the others.

The major division was on religious grounds. The Abbasid dynasty, which had been taken over by the Seljuks and which ruled from Baghdad, were Sunni Muslims (see page 17). They had invaded Syria and driven out the Fatimids, who were Shi'ite Muslims whose dynasty ruled from Cairo in Egypt.

ZENGI

The presence of the crusader states, however, meant that all the Muslims now had a common enemy. To regain their lands they had to unite. This did not happen overnight, but by about 1130 there was a degree of unity with the rise of an important leader in the person of Zengi, the atabeg of Mosul. Zengi began to promote the idea of a holy war, or jihad. Historians disagree about Zengi's motives, however; many think that the jihad was not the sole or even the main aim of his policy. His aim was to found a kingdom stretching from Armenia in the north to Egypt in the south. In 1128 he had become emir (ruler) of Aleppo, thus uniting it with Mosul. From Aleppo, his first goal was Damascus, a powerful and important state. He conquered all the Islamic towns to the east of the Orontes river but in both 1135 and in 1139 he failed to secure Damascus. In fact, the Damascenes appealed to the king of Jerusalem for help as they feared the expansion of Zengi's power and his reputation for harshness.

He then turned his attention to the north and, in December 1144, was able to take the crusader city of Edessa, while its ruler, Count Joscelin II, was absent from it. Thus the first crusader city to be gained became the first to be lost. This caused considerable consternation in the west and led to the second crusade. Zengi gained a reputation as a champion of Islam. The caliph of Baghdad conferred on him the titles of the Ornament of Islam, the Auxiliary of the Commander of the Faithful and the Divinely Aided King. In only a few years he had halved the territory of the Latin states of the north, but in September 1146 he was murdered by a slave while he lay in a drunken stupor.

NUREDDIN

On the death of Zengi his territories were divided and his second son, Nureddin, became the governor of Aleppo. His aim was to carry on the jihad against the Frankish states in Syria. Almost immediately after Zengi's death Joscelin attempted to retake Edessa, but Nureddin defeated him and massacred thousands of the Christians native to the city. A few months later, the leaders of the second crusade besieged Damascus and its ruler appealed to Nureddin for help (see page 40). He advanced to the south and the crusaders abandoned the siege. An alliance was made between Damascus and Nureddin. In 1149 he defeated Raymond of Poitiers, prince of Antioch, a man with a reputation as a fearless warrior, and took most of the territory belonging to Antioch, although not the city itself. In 1154 he took Damascus itself, which he saw as the key to the control of Syria and the Latin states. The borders of Muslim Syria had been extended to Mosul, Harran and, to the north, as far as the Taurus mountains. The Franks were now facing a Muslim Syria united under one leader.

Nureddin had carefully developed the idea of the jihad. He stressed that it was essential to fight against the Franks until they left or died. He emphasised that Jerusalem was a special holy city to the Muslims and that the Muslims should be united politically. He created schools and appointed teachers to teach the ideas of Sunni Islam and the jihad. He introduced the *hadiths*, records of the words and behaviour of the prophet Mohammed, to Syria. He also developed an efficient propaganda machine to spread his ideas through poetry, songs, letters and treatises. He developed a courier system and used carrier pigeons to take information and orders. He built up an efficient administration system and the taxes he raised enabled him to have a sumptuous court and a strong army.

EGYPT

In 1153 the Franks, under Baldwin III, had captured the city of Ascalon, which opened the way to Egypt in the south. Egypt was a land of great wealth and also the land of the Shi'ite Fatimid dynasty. It looked ripe for intervention as its government had been weakened by the fact that the last adult caliph had died in 1149 and the next three caliphs in the following eleven years had been children. Real power rested with the office of vizier and various emirs competed for this office. If Nureddin could gain Egypt he could surround the Latin states with Muslim-held territory. He could also extend the Sunni faith into Shi'ite territory. On the other hand, the Franks also needed control of Egypt in order to avoid being surrounded and to use its wealth.

In 1164 Shawar, a vizier of upper Egypt who had taken refuge with Nureddin, convinced him to send a mission to Egypt to re-establish a Sunni government there. Nureddin sent forces to Egypt led by a Kurdish lieutenant by the name of Shurkuh. Shurkuh was victorious, the Sunni government was restored and Shawar regained his office of vizier. However, Shawar then disagreed with Shurkuh and sent to the Franks for help. Amalric, king of Jerusalem, led an army into Egypt to face the forces of Shurkuh and the nephew he had taken with him – a man by the name of Saladin.

Saladin

THE VIZIER OF EGYPT

In 1167 Amalric, king of Jerusalem, advanced as far as Cairo in order to help Shawar. He forced Shurkuh, Nureddin's lieutenant, who was trying to take control of Egypt, to retreat. Shawar promised Amalric a tribute of gold from Egypt if he would leave a garrison of soldiers there and return to Jerusalem. This he did but in 1168 he invaded Egypt again, this time without an invitation. Shawar then appealed to Shurkuh for help and the Franks were heavily defeated and driven out. Saladin, Shurkuh's nephew, then arrested Shawar and put him to death. Shurkuh became vizier but within three months he too was dead (some historians say that he was poisoned, or assassinated by Saladin).

Saladin thus became the vizier of Egypt and took over the government. In the name of Nureddin he abolished the Fatimid caliphate, announced that Egypt was returned to the Abbasid caliphate and founded state schools to teach the Sunni religion. The Egyptians rallied to Saladin, who took the title of *malik* (king). This had all been done in the name of Nureddin but, in subjecting Egypt, with all its abundant wealth and resources, to himself, Saladin became Nureddin's rival. Nureddin decided to invade Egypt to remove Saladin but he died on 15 May 1174.

SALADIN AND THE ZENGIDS

After the death of Nureddin, Saladin himself set about the attempt to unite Egypt with Syria. He was resisted, however, by the Zengids (the followers of Zengi and Nureddin who held Aleppo and Mosul). They considered him to be a usurper. He was also threatened by the Assassins, a Shia Muslim sect that tried to murder him. Not surprisingly, the Franks also tried to prevent Saladin defeating the Zengids as they realised that, if he did so, his resources and forces would be invincible. They therefore fought against him to divert him from the north. The balance of power shifted in Saladin's favour in 1176. A huge Seljuk army, led by Kilij Arslan, defeated the Byzantine emperor, Manuel I Comnenus, at Myriocephalum and virtually wiped out his army. The Franks could not now call on the Byzantine emperor for assistance.

SALADIN AND THE FRANKS

Saladin continued to attack and the Franks, although holding on to their territory, suffered losses. They eventually made a truce with Saladin in 1180. The truce was broken in 1181 by Reynaud de Chatillon, lord of Transjordan. His castles of Moab and Montreal controlled the road from Damascus to Mecca, which passed through Egypt and was crucial to Saladin. Reynaud plundered a very rich caravan and refused to return the booty to Saladin, despite being

---

THE KEY ISSUES

- What factors brought about Muslim recovery?
- How was the kingdom of the Franks weakened?

THE KEY SKILLS

Analysis
Chronology
Recording
Assessment
Explanation
Interpretation

---

1. Complete the flow chart showing the stages of Muslim unity. Include the second and third crusades and highlight them so that you can see where they occurred and what the Muslim situation was at the time.
2. Shade on your map, in a different colour, the Muslim areas united under Saladin.
3. Research the life of Saladin and answer the question: *What qualities enabled him to keep an army in the field for such a long time?*

It is difficult to see the overall picture of Muslim recovery unless it is dealt with in the same place. This chapter, therefore, covers the topic up to the battle of Hattin in 1187, which led to the third crusade. In chapter 7 we will go back and look at the events of the second crusade, and then continue in chapter 8 to look at the third crusade.

ordered to do so by Baldwin IV. Saladin therefore attacked Samaria. He accused the Zengids of being in alliance with the Franks and in June 1183 he took Aleppo, which was the last link in the chain of Syrian–Egyptian unity. His lands then stretched from Yemen to the eastern borders of Tunisia. Reynaud de Chatillon responded by pillaging Egyptian and Arab ports and marching on Medina. This attack on a holy city was seen as an outrage by the Muslims, and Saladin turned it to his advantage by making himself the avenger of Islam. He captured and killed every member of the expedition except for Reynaud, who managed to escape.

In September 1183 Saladin destroyed Galilee and seized several castles, but the Franks defended their territory and Saladin was forced to retreat. Inevitably the Franks were hampered by a lack of provisions and Saladin attacked them both by land and by sea. In 1185 he granted them a four-year truce. He had united Syria and Egypt under his control but had failed to take the Frankish states. It was the Franks, however, who were left in a weak position. They had an army of no more than a thousand knights who could not be replaced, whereas Saladin had a huge army and could call on others if his men were lost in battle. Saladin had also rebuilt the Egyptian fleet and blocked the Palestinian ports so that the Franks could not bring in supplies. He was even cultivating relations with the Italian republics in the hope of buying swords from them. Saladin's only weak point was that he did not have a standing army. His soldiers were assembled for each campaign and then returned to their local emirs. To keep an army in the field for a long time was a major problem.

THE FALL OF JERUSALEM

The truce was broken once again by Reynaud de Chatillon. Saladin's empire was at its height and the kingdom of Jerusalem was split into factions, isolated and weak. Saladin mobilised some 12 000 cavalry and besieged the castles of Moab and Montreal. In 1187 he crossed the river Jordan to lay siege to Tiberias. In the same year he met and destroyed the Frankish army at the battle of Hattin and captured the relic of the True Cross that they carried into battle with them. He then went on to take Jerusalem. Only the port of Tyre remained to the kingdom of Jerusalem. This event was the direct cause of the third crusade during which, according to legend, Saladin, the champion of Islam, was to meet his match in the champion of the Christian world, Richard I of England.

Two useful books on the life of Saladin are P. Newby, *Saladin in his Time* (Faber & Faber, 1983), and H. A. R. Gibb, *The Life of Saladin, from the Works of Imad ad-Din and Baha ad-Din* (Clarendon Press, 1971).

'Saladin took over Nureddin's program in full (including marrying his widow), but on an even larger scale. He came very close to succeeding … Saladin was the strongest personality of his time. His courage and loyalty evoked both admiration and jealousy in enemy and ally alike.'

Georges Tate, The Crusades and the Holy Land, 1996

Reynaud de Chatillon

Reynaud (sometimes called Reginald) de Chatillon was the younger son of a French count who came to the Holy Land with the second crusade but did not return. He entered the service of Baldwin III and in 1153 married Constance, the widow of Raymond of Antioch. He quarrelled with the patriarch of Antioch, who disapproved of the marriage. He plundered Cyprus because the Byzantine emperor did not pay him for his help in Cilicia. He rustled cattle from Armenian and Syrian Christians and was imprisoned for 16 years by the governor of Aleppo. Constance died while he was in captivity and so, on his release, he married the widow of Milon de Plancy and became lord of the great castle of Krak in Moab, near the Dead Sea. From here he raided caravans travelling from Egypt to Damascus, regardless of truces. Trevor John describes him as 'part adventurer, part brigand, part religious fanatic' (*The Crusades*, 1972).

THE KEY ISSUES

- Why did the pope call for a second crusade?
- Why did kings and nobles respond to the call for the second crusade?
- Why were relationships with the Byzantine empire strained?

THE KEY SKILLS

Assessment
Explanation
Analysis
Forming hypotheses

Bernard of Clairvaux

'It is difficult now to look back across the centuries and appreciate the tremendous impact of his personality on all who knew him. The fire of his eloquence has been quenched in the written words that survive. As a theologian and a controversialist he now appears rigid and a little crude and unkind. But from the day in 1115 when he was appointed Abbot of Clairvaux, till his death nearly 40 years later, he was the dominant influence in the religious and political life of western Europe.'

Stephen Runciman, The Crusades, 1951

Read your texts to find out more about the second crusade and then answer the questions posed in the Key Issues.

A Crusade Led by Kings

CONCERN IN THE WEST

The fall of Edessa to Zengi in 1144 caused great concern, both in the Holy Land and in the west. The north-eastern flank of the crusader states now lay open to attack. King Fulk had died in 1143, leaving his wife, Melisende, to administer the kingdom for his son, Baldwin III, who was only a child. She appealed to the pope, the recently elected Eugenius III, for help. He issued a papal bull (*Quantum praedecessores*) calling on Christians to go to the rescue of their brothers in Outremer, but this had little effect. Concerned over the lack of papal authority that this showed, he in turn appealed to the man who had done much to promote his election, Bernard of Clairvaux.

BERNARD OF CLAIRVAUX

Bernard addressed the nobility of France at Vézélay on 31 March 1146. They had been summoned there by the French king Louis VII. Louis was a pious man and it is thought that he may have felt the need to atone for a massacre committed in his name at Vitry sur Marne. Louis had earlier tried to get an expedition together to go to the east at his Christmas court held at Bourges in 1145 but this had been unsuccessful.

Bernard of Clairvaux was fifty-six years old in 1146 and at the height of his fame. He had enormous influence in both the political and religious life of the time. At Vézélay the cathedral could not contain all the people who had come to hear Bernard and he had to preach to them in a field outside the town. He read the papal bull to them and then preached to them himself. There is no record of what he said at Vézélay but he later wrote many letters urging Christians to take part in the crusade. From these we learn that he laid a much greater emphasis on the crusade as a work of penance for the salvation of the soul than Urban had done in 1095. He spoke specifically to the knightly classes. He advised them to learn from the lessons of the first crusade by making sure that they took time to prepare so that they could go together in good order. The response was immediate and overwhelming. So many people took the cross that Bernard had to cut crosses from his own habit because they had run out of cloth.

CONRAD III OF GERMANY

It is thought that the pope did not want the German emperor, Conrad, to take part in the crusade as he needed his help to fight the Normans in Italy. However, popular preachers began to spread the message in Germany. This led to massacres of the Jews, which Bernard had been anxious to prevent, and so he went to Germany to deal, in particular, with a Cistercian monk by the name of Radulf (or Rudolf) who had been stirring up enthusiasm for the crusade and fanning the flames of anti-semitism. Bernard preached before the king at Frankfurt in November 1146 and again at Speyer at

Christmas. Conrad and many of his nobles took the cross. Thus it was that the forces gathering to go to the east were led in this second crusade by kings – the king of France and the emperor of Germany, accompanied by many of their greatest nobles.

In 1147 the armies of the two kings set off separately across Europe for Constantinople, roughly following the route of the first crusaders. Like the first crusaders they met with disasters and trials along the way. They both had to pass through Byzantine territory and cross over the Bosphorus at Constantinople. As the armies were nearing Constantinople, Manuel Comnenus, the Byzantine emperor, who feared this new crusading army, made peace with the Seljuks of Anatolia. This looked like deliberate hostility to the crusaders. Manuel Comnenus ushered the crusading armies over the Bosphorus as quickly as possible, giving them only guides and advice. Conrad was the first to leave and at Nicaea he split his army into two parts. All went well until he and his force reached Dorylaeum, where the first crusaders had won their first victory. They were attacked suddenly by the Seljuk army before they could organise resistance. Only Conrad and a small remnant survived and made their way back to Nicaea. The other part of his army was routed at Laodicaea, and many of the survivors died of hunger and thirst after the battle.

LOUIS VII

When Louis reached Nicaea he learned what had become of Conrad's army and asked the remnant of the German forces to join him. Conrad, however, fell ill at Ephesus and went back to Constantinople. The French fared little better than the Germans, being constantly short of water and food and at the mercy of the weather and Turkish attacks. They blamed the Byzantines, accusing them of deliberately misguiding them. The Byzantines blamed the westerners, thought of them as barbarians and resented the fact that they had brought Turkish attacks on their towns. At Attalia Louis VII, his nobles and most of his cavalry sailed to Syria. As there were insufficient ships, the rest of his forces had to make their way on foot. Only a few of these survived to reach Antioch.

St Bernard of Clairvaux, in the white robes of the Cistercians, preaches the second crusade at Vézélay in 1146, in the presence of Louis VII

From Letter no. 363 of Bernard of Clairvaux:

'What is it but a unique and wonderful act of divine generosity when the Almighty God treats murderers, thieves, adulterers, perjurers, and criminals of all kinds as though they were men of righteousness and worthy to be called to his service. Do not hesitate. God is good. He pretends to be in debt so that he can repay those who take up arms on his behalf with the forgiveness of sins and with eternal glory ... O mighty soldier, O man of war, you now have a cause for which you can fight without endangering your soul; a cause in which to win is glorious and for which to die is but gain ...

Or are you a shrewd businessman, a man quick to see the profits of this world? If you are, I can offer you a splendid bargain. Do not miss this opportunity. Take the sign of the cross. At once you will have indulgences for all the sins which you confess with a contrite heart. It does not cost you much to buy and if you wear it with humility you will find that it is the kingdom of heaven.'

William of Tyre on the Byzantine guides:

'The guides ... led by the malice in the Greek race and also by their customary hatred of the Christians, acted treacherously. Either commanded by their master or because bribed by the Turks they purposely led the legions by unfrequented routes and drew them into places which offered the enemy favourable opportunities to attack.'

THE KEY ISSUES

- Why did the leaders from the east and the west disagree?
- Why did the second crusade fail?

THE KEY SKILLS

Analysis
Evaluation
Interpretation
Explanation

Answer the question:
Why was the second crusade a failure?

Damascus

Damascus was a Muslim city, ruled by atabegs, who prized their independence. The crusaders had tried to capture the city after the first crusade but they had failed. They could not afford to have Damascus as a constant threat to peace on their eastern borders and so they made an alliance to live alongside each other peacefully, to create an area where both sides could pasture their flocks and share the revenues. The knights and barons who later came out to the Holy Land from western Europe were horrified at what they saw was an intolerable compromise with the infidel. They did not understand the strategic importance of an alliance with Damascus, and this accounts for many of the mistakes made in the second crusade.

A Debacle in Outremer

ELEANOR AND ANTIOCH

Louis VII's wife, Eleanor, had accompanied him on the crusade. On arriving at Antioch, they were greeted by Eleanor's uncle, Raymond of Antioch. Raymond entertained the royal party in style and luxury. Louis had to decide how best to deploy his forces but the rulers of the Latin states wanted him to do different things: Raymond of Antioch wanted him to attack Aleppo, Joscelin of Edessa wanted him to retake Edessa and Raymond of Tripoli wanted him to help to capture the castle of Montferrand, which was of strategic importance. Louis also had domestic troubles. There were rumours of an affair between Eleanor and Raymond. When Louis eventually decided that he should go to Jerusalem, Eleanor wanted to stay in Antioch and divorce him. Louis forced Eleanor to go to Jerusalem with him. In doing so he lost the co-operation of Raymond of Antioch and, later, he lost his wife as well, as they divorced.

A CONFERENCE

Conrad had been taken to Jerusalem by Byzantine ship and he met Louis there. After fulfilling their vows as pilgrims, they went to a conference at Acre with the king of Jerusalem and some of the leaders in Outremer to decide the best plan of action. We do not know who said what at Acre but we do know that they came to a decision which various historians have described as 'ridiculous' (Mayer), 'utter folly' (Runciman) and 'unimaginable stupidity' (Bridge): they decided to attack Damascus. Damascus was of strategic importance as it separated the Egyptian Muslims from those in Syria and the east, but the Damascenes were extremely wary of the threat of Nureddin in the north and had made an alliance with the Franks. The local barons would have known this but the westerners may have been idealistic and unwilling to tolerate any infidel in the Latin states.

DAMASCUS

Damascus was an oasis city, with orchards surrounding a large part of it. In July 1148 the largest Christian army that the Franks had ever put in the field encamped in the orchards, where they had plenty to eat and, perhaps more importantly, to drink. The governor of Damascus had no choice but to send messengers to Nureddin asking for his help. The crusaders did well at first, defeating the Muslim army and forcing it back into the city, but they did not press their advantage and attack the walls when they could. Reinforcements arrived for the Muslims and guerrilla fighters took advantage of the fruit trees in the orchards to harass the crusader troops. The leaders then took yet another disastrous decision and moved their troops away from the orchards to another part of the city, where not only were the walls stronger but also there was no water. Chroniclers put this decision down to disagreements and misunderstandings between the Palestinian and the western barons. Only four days after they had arrived they were forced to retreat in ignominy. Their campaign had only succeeded in persuading the Damascenes to ally themselves with Nureddin and, ultimately, in allowing him to take possession of Damascus in 1154.

Bitter recriminations followed the disaster at Damascus. Later in the summer of 1148 Conrad left Outremer and signed a treaty with the emperor Manuel Comnenus, promising to help him against the Normans, especially Roger of Sicily. When Louis VII heard this he made an alliance with Roger of Sicily and left the Latin states in a Sicilian ship to go to meet Roger in Italy. There, Roger persuaded him to help promote a crusade against Byzantium. When Louis returned to France he persuaded Bernard of Clairvaux to preach against the Byzantines but the pope and Conrad refused to have anything to do with a crusade against Christians. The crusade did not happen; the idea, however, had taken root.

FAILURE AND HUMILIATION

The second crusade had been called by the pope, it had been preached by the greatest preacher of the day, it had been led by kings and great nobles and yet it was an abject failure. Bernard of Clairvaux was deeply humiliated. He had promised forgiveness of sins to those who took part and now he could only see the defeat as a judgement of God against the sins of man. The monarchies of Germany and France had been weakened by the absence of their kings and nobles, and Louis VII had also lost his wife. The divisions between the Greek and the Latin churches had widened. Suspicion and distrust had become rife, not only between Greek and Latin, but also between the rulers of the Latin states and the western barons. For the next forty years there was little interest in crusading. The only positive lesson that appeared to have been learned was that, if one was intending to go to the Holy Land, it was better to go by sea.

The disaster at Damascus

From the writings of William of Tyre:

'Certain of our nobles ... on assurance of receiving a great sum of money [were persuaded by the Damascenes] to endeavour to raise the siege ... Their wicked suggestions persuaded the king and the pilgrim princes ... to leave the orchards and move the armies to the opposite side of the city ...

They soon perceived ... that this position was far away from the abundant fruit and convenient supply of water, and as food was already beginning to ail they realised that treachery had been at work ...

To return to the position they had left seemed difficult, in fact, impossible. For as soon as the Christians departed, the enemy ... immediately entered in and established even stronger defences than before.'

From the Damascus Chronicle:

'When the Moslems learned this, and the signs of the retreat of the Franks became clear to them, they moved out to attack them, and hastened towards them, pursuing them with arrows, so that they slew a large number of men, horses and animals in their rear files. In the remains of their camp, moreover, and along their highroads there were found such uncountable quantities of burial pits of their slain and of their magnificent horses, that there were stenches from their corpses that almost overcame the birds in the air.'

THE KEY ISSUES

- Why did the third crusade take place?
- What were the motives of the leaders?
- How was the crusade planned and financed?
- How did relations with Byzantium change during the crusade?

THE KEY SKILLS

Analysis
Interpretation
Assessment
Recording

Vassal – a person who holds lands from a superior, in return for military service

John Gillingham has written two very readable books about Richard I: *Richard I* (Hambledon Press, 1989) and *Richard the Lionheart* (Hambledon Press, 1994). Also very readable is Jim Bradbury, *Philip Augustus, King of France, 1180–1223* (Longman, 1998).

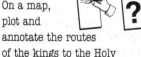

1. On a map, plot and annotate the routes of the kings to the Holy Land.
2. Read more about the personalities of Philip II (Augustus) of France and Richard I of England. Make notes from your reading.

A New Crusade

THE KINGS RESPOND

The western world was shocked to the core when Jerusalem fell to Saladin in 1187. The Frankish army had been all but wiped out at the battle of Hattin, the Muslims had captured the relic of the True Cross and of the kingdom of Jerusalem only the port of Tyre was left to the Franks. To the north, in the other Latin states, only the cities of Antioch and Tripoli remained – the surrounding territory had fallen into Muslim hands. Many in the west had relatives in Outremer who had lost their lands or their lives. This time it was scarcely necessary for the pope to proclaim a crusade. William II of Sicily was the first to respond, followed by Henry II of England, the emperor Frederick Barbarossa of Germany and Philip II of France. Henry II died before he could fulfil his vow and his place was taken by his son Richard I, known as the Lionheart.

Despite this over-abundance of kings and princes, there was little in the way of unity or a co-ordinated strategy. William II died shortly after sending a fleet to the Holy Land. The Sicilians and the Germans acted independently of each other. The French and the English formed one expedition but they did not trust each other and, for Philip, the main concern was to limit Richard's power in France. At this period Richard held far more land in France than did Philip, although technically he was Philip's vassal. Philip and Richard both levied taxes on their kingdoms to pay for the crusade and, before they set out, they agreed to share any booty that was captured. The German contingent was required to take enough money with them to last for two years.

FREDERICK BARBAROSSA

Frederick Barbarossa was the first to set out in May 1189, leading the largest single crusading army ever to leave Europe. He was an able and well-respected ruler and soldier and had made his preparations carefully. He travelled over land, having previously written to the king of Hungary, the Byzantine emperor and the Seljuk sultan through whose lands he intended to march. All went well until the army reached Byzantine territory, where they were harassed by bandits. This caused resentment against the Byzantines. The emperor, Isaac Angelus, panicked at the approach of such a large army. Frederick sent ambassadors to make arrangements for his army to cross the Bosphorus but Isaac threw them into prison. Frederick's reaction was to ask for the pope's blessing on a crusade against the Byzantines and to plan an attack on Constantinople. Isaac released the ambassadors and made peace.

In the spring of 1190 Barbarossa marched into Turkish territory. The Seljuk sultan of Rum had promised him safe conduct but his son, who was a son-in-law of Saladin, led attacks against the Christians. Frederick won a major victory near Iconium in May 1190, and the sultan apologised for the actions of his son and restored safe passage for the crusaders through his territory. In June 1190, in mysterious circumstances, Frederick Barbarossa drowned in the river Saleph. This had a demoralising effect on his army, so that many went home the way they had come. Some struggled on to Antioch with the body of the emperor, which they buried there, and Leopold of Austria assumed command of the very much depleted force that was left.

PHILIP AND RICHARD

On 4 July 1190 both Richard and Philip left Vézélay to go by sea to the Holy Land. They went by separate routes but met in Sicily. Richard's sister, Joanna, was the widow of William II of Sicily, and she accused William's heir, Tancred, of treating her badly. Richard therefore attacked and took Messina and made a treaty with Tancred in return for gold. Both Philip and Richard wintered in Sicily and then left separately. Philip went straight to Tyre but Richard's ship was blown off course to Cyprus. Cyprus, which was part of the Byzantine empire, was ruled by Isaac Comnenus, a pretender to the Byzantine throne. He imprisoned some of Richard's men who had been shipwrecked; in retaliation for this Richard conquered the island and took booty from Isaac Comnenus. This was to prove a very useful acquisition in the future but at the time it did nothing to improve relations between the English and the French, and between the western Christians and the Byzantines. Richard arrived in the Holy Land seven weeks after Philip, at the beginning of June 1191.

THE CAMP AT ACRE

In 1188, when Saladin had captured Jerusalem, he had freed the king of Jerusalem, Guy de Lusignan, on condition that he left the country. Guy had sworn an oath to this effect but, after he had been set free, he asked the church to release him from it as he had made it under duress to a Muslim. He then went to Tyre, which was occupied by Conrad of Montferrat, a rival claimant to the throne. Conrad refused him entry, however, so Guy took what remained of a Frankish army to Acre and began to besiege it. Saladin and his forces had not been able to dislodge him so they surrounded the besiegers.

Acre thus became the centre of Christian resistance against the Moslems and it was to that city that Richard and Philip took their forces. The siege lasted for another two months, during which time both Richard and Philip fell ill. Eventually, however, the Muslims in the city offered to surrender, pay a large sum in gold, release 1500 prisoners and return the True Cross in return for their lives. Saladin had to honour this agreement.

THE KEY ISSUES

- How did the domestic problems of the kings affect their conduct of the crusade?
- What sort of general was Richard I?
- Why did Richard I fail to regain Jerusalem?
- What did the third crusade achieve?

THE KEY SKILLS

Analysis
Interpretation
Explanation
Assessment
Evaluation

Answer the question:
What did the third crusade achieve?

Some notes on Jerusalem

Guy de Lusignan had claimed the throne of Jerusalem in the right of his wife, Sibylla, sister of Baldwin IV. He was supported by barons from the west. The Palestinian barons supported the claim of Humphrey de Toron, one of their number who was married to Isabella, the younger sister of Baldwin IV. When Humphrey died, Isabella married Conrad de Montferrat and he claimed the throne in her right.

In order to appreciate the difficulties that Richard I would have faced in holding Jerusalem, had he captured it, look back at chapter 6 to remind yourself of the position and extent of the lands united in the Muslim cause. Jerusalem was the capital city for religious and emotional reasons, rather than economic ones. The ports were the most important places for the survival of the Latin states.

Richard and Saladin

THE CAMP AT ACRE

After Acre had been won the crusaders began to argue amongst themselves. Both Guy de Lusignan and Conrad de Montferrat had a claim to be the king of Jerusalem and each had their party of supporters. Richard supported Guy and Philip supported Conrad. Leopold of Austria wanted to be treated as an equal of the French and English kings, so he ran up his standard in the city, next to Richard's. This meant that he had a claim to some of the booty from the city. Richard and Philip, however, had agreed to share booty between them and tore Leopold's flag down. Leopold never forgot this insult and it was to have disastrous consequences for Richard on his return from the crusade.

Early in August 1191 Philip went home to France, leaving his forces under the command of the duke of Burgundy. This left Richard in sole control of the crusading forces. He was acknowledged by all, even Saladin, to be a superb military commander but he now had the worry that Philip was back in France plotting to take over his land there.

ARSUF

Saladin was having problems holding a large Muslim army in the field. His soldiers had been fighting with him for nearly three years, and mutinies and quarrels were breaking out. He concentrated on holding Jerusalem and threatening the crusaders' supply lines in the interior of the country. Richard realised that if he was to take Jerusalem he first of all needed the port of Jaffa (the nearest to Jerusalem) as a base to bring in supplies. He marched south from Acre, using the fleet and the sea to protect the right flank of the army. In On 7 September 1191 Saladin tried to break the crusader army at Arsuf, north of Jaffa, but Richard kept to his order of battle until his archers had exhausted the Muslims. Then he ordered the charge of the knights and the Muslims were unable to offer any resistance.

JERUSALEM

Richard took Jaffa but it was Jerusalem that the crusaders wanted. He advanced towards Jerusalem and got within twelve miles of it, but he realised that if he went on and tried to take it he would have been caught in a trap outside the city by any relief Muslim force coming from Egypt. He withdrew to Ascalon, therefore, which had been destroyed by Saladin, and began to refortify it. Here he heard that Philip II of France and his own brother John were intriguing against him in the west. He needed to get home urgently. In June 1192 he advanced on Jerusalem yet again, and again withdrew as he realised that he could not take and hold on to the Holy City. His army withdrew to Acre and Saladin captured Jaffa. As soon as Richard heard this, he sailed to Jaffa with just a few knights. There he waded through the water to the beach, cleared the town of Muslims and beat off an attack by Saladin.

Richard and Saladin realised that neither of them could inflict a decisive defeat on the other and so on 2 September 1192 they made a three-year truce. By its terms the Christians were to retain control of the coast from Tyre to Jaffa. The Muslims did, however, agree that pilgrims could visit Jerusalem. Ascalon was handed back to the Muslims but only after its fortifications had been razed to the ground.

AFTERMATH

Richard left the Holy Land on 9 October 1192. Conrad de Montferrat was made king of Jerusalem and Guy de Lusignan was given Cyprus as compensation. Conrad's victory was short-lived: he was assassinated before he could be crowned. Within a few days his widow, Isabella, married Henry of Champagne, who was proclaimed king. Richard was shipwrecked on his way home and forced to travel through Austria. Despite travelling in disguise, he was recognised and imprisoned by Leopold, who had never forgotten the incident of the standard in Acre. Richard was not released until 1194 after the payment of a huge ransom. Saladin died in 1193, while Richard was in captivity. Richard himself died in 1199, fighting to recover his lands from Philip II.

The third crusade was undoubtedly the greatest effort made by the west to conquer Syria and to establish the crusader states permanently, with Jerusalem as their capital. However, they had failed to retake Jerusalem. Their cause had been weakened by quarrels and dissension within their ranks; in Saladin and his army they had literally met their match. There was no decisive victory on either side.

However, by refusing to overstretch his forces and attempt to retake Jerusalem, Richard I had ensured that the coastal strip remained in Frankish hands. Cyprus was also of great value, as supplies and reinforcements could be sent from there in a crisis. The crusader states were to continue for another hundred years or so. The Italian maritime cities grew wealthy out of trade with the east but westerners realised that Outremer was not a land flowing with milk and honey. If material gain was the motive for crusaders then it was to be looked for elsewhere – in Egypt, perhaps, or in Constantinople.

A 15th-century portrait of Saladin

Richard I

Baha ad-Din, a member of Saladin's entourage, on Richard I:

'The king of England was a very powerful man among the Franks, a man of great courage and spirit. He had fought great battles, and showed a burning passion for war. His kingdom and standing were inferior to those of the French king, but his wealth, reputation and valour were greater ...

The Frankish rulers had for a long time been telling us that he was coming, and those of them that had safe-conducts and could contact our side said that they had been waiting for his arrival to put into effect their plan to besiege the city with new vigour. The king was indeed a man of wisdom, experience, courage and energy. His arrival put fear into the hearts of the Moslems, but the Sultan [Saladin] met the panic with firmness and faith in God.'

Joinville (John, lord of Joinville), from one of the great noble families of France, was writing in the 13th century. Here he describes Richard's turning back from Jerusalem:

'One of the knights called out: "My lord! My lord! Come over here and I will show you Jerusalem!" On hearing this, the king had thrown his emblazoned tunic over his eyes, and, weeping bitterly, had cried to our Saviour: "Dear Lord, I pray Thee to suffer me not to see Thy Holy City since I cannot deliver it from the hands of Thy enemies!"'

A soldier in the English army describes Richard's leaving the Holy Land:

'All night the ship ran on her way by the light of the stars, and when morning dawned, the king looked back with yearning eyes upon the land which he had left, and after long meditation prayed aloud ... "O holy land, I commend thee to God, and if His heavenly grace shall grant me so long to live ... I hope ... to be some day a saviour to thee." With these words he urged the sailors to spread their canvas to the winds.'

THE KEY ISSUES

- Why was the fourth crusade proclaimed?
- Why were the crusaders diverted from the Holy Land?
- Were the motives of the crusaders religious or commercial?

THE KEY SKILLS

Analysis
Assessment
Explanation
Interpretation
Forming hypotheses
Evaluation

1. Start to make a flow chart showing the events of the fourth crusade.
2. Answer the question: *Why were the crusaders diverted from the Holy Land?*

William of Tyre's view of the Greek Christians

'For they having separated insolently from the Church of Rome, in their boundless arrogance looked upon everyone who did not follow their foolish traditions as a heretic. It was they themselves ... who deserved the name of heretics, because they had either created or followed new and pernicious beliefs contrary to the Roman church.'

Complications and Diversions

THE BACKGROUND

In 1095, when Urban had called for help for the east, he had done so at the request of the Byzantine emperor. At that time the Greek church of the east and the Latin church of the west were separate. Far from uniting them in a common cause, however, the crusades had only made the situation worse. The Latins thought that the Greeks were treacherous, and they envied the wealth of Constantinople. The Greeks thought of the crusaders and the Muslims alike as political enemies and resented, in particular, the Venetians who were taking more and more of the empire's trade. Venice, Genoa and Pisa were great rivals for trade in the east and Byzantine emperors appeared to be favouring Genoa and Pisa in an attempt to limit the power of the Venetians. The emperor Manuel Comnenus, who reigned from 1143 to 1180, had favoured the Latins and many western Europeans had settled in Constantinople. After his death resentment of the westerners had grown; in 1182 there was a terrible massacre of the Latin occupants of Constantinople by the Greeks.

INNOCENT III

Innocent III was elected pope in 1198. He wanted to make the whole world recognise the papacy in Rome as the supreme authority in both religious and secular matters. As soon as he became pope he began to speak of a new crusade, entirely under his control. Experience had proved that the only successful crusade, the first, was the one in which kings had had no involvement. He therefore directed his appeal to the knights. He sent preachers into France and Germany with the most remarkable offer of forgiveness of sins to date in exchange for participation in the crusade. According to Villehardouin, a knight who took part in the crusade, he promised: 'All those who take the Cross and remain for one year in the service of God in the army shall obtain remission of any sins they have committed, provided they have confessed them.'

THE RESPONSE

In 1199, at a tournament held in Écry, Thibaut, count of Champagne, took the cross. Other nobles from northern France joined him. However, they had no means of getting their armies to the Holy Land except by sea. The route that previous crusaders had taken was closed to them because of the weakness of the Byzantine empire. In 1202, therefore, a delegation was sent to Venice to negotiate transport. The cost was set at 85 000 marks. The crusade was to go to Cairo in Egypt to attack the Muslims to the south of the Latin states. Meanwhile, Count Thibaut died and the crusaders chose a new leader to replace him – Boniface de Montferrat, a man with a fearsome reputation.

VENETIAN AMBITIONS

Some of the crusaders distrusted the Venetians and decided to make their own way to the Holy Land. The others could not raise the 85 000 marks from the troops that had assembled at the camp in Venice. The doge of Venice, Enrico Dandolo, had an agenda of his own. He wanted Venice to control the Byzantine empire so that the Venetians could have undisputed rights to its wealth and trade, totally excluding Genoa and Pisa. He proposed that payment of the debt could be postponed if the crusaders first of all helped him to capture the town of Zara. This was an important port on the eastern side of the Adriatic, but it was also a Christian city. The leaders had little choice but to agree, and Enrico Dandolo took the cross; the rank and file of the army must have thought that they were, at last, off to the Holy Land to fight the infidel.

Innocent III tried to prevent the attack on Zara, but the majority of the leaders decided to go ahead: they needed the booty in order to finance their expedition. Zara was taken and plundered on 24 November 1202, and Innocent excommunicated the whole army. Later, when he realised that the crusaders had had little choice in the matter, he forgave them, but not the Venetians. The suggestion was then put to the leaders that, in return for money and men, they should help the Greek prince Alexius to gain the Byzantine throne. His father, Isaac Angelus, by all accounts an ineffectual ruler, had lost the throne to his brother. He had been blinded and thrown into prison and his son, Alexius, had taken refuge with his sister. Enrico Dandolo was very much in favour of this plan, in view of his city's hatred of the Byzantine empire, but some of the crusaders could not bring themselves to contemplate another attack on a Christian city and they left the main body of the army and made their own way to the Holy Land.

Villehardouin writes about Enrico Dandolo taking the cross in Venice:

'"If you will consent to my [Dandolo] taking the cross so that I can protect and guide you ... then I shall go to live or die with you and with the pilgrims." On hearing the Doge's words, all the Venetians cried out with one accord: "We beg you in God's name to take the cross and go with us." At that moment the hearts of all those present, French and Venetians alike, were deeply moved, and many a tear was shed out of sympathy for this good and worthy man who would have had so much reason to stay behind. For he was very old and ... totally blind, having lost his sight through a wound in the head ... They sewed the cross on to the front of his great cotton cap, because he wished everyone to see it.'

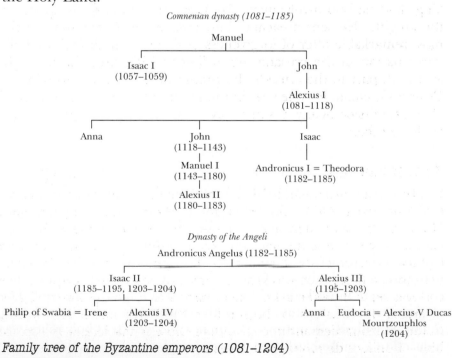

Family tree of the Byzantine emperors (1081–1204)

THE KEY ISSUE

- Why did the crusaders attack Constantinople?

THE KEY SKILLS

Analysis
Assessment
Explanation
Interpretation
Forming hypotheses
Recording

The sack of Constantinople

Nicetas Choniates, a Greek nobleman in the city of Constantinople during the attack, describes what he saw:

'When the enemy saw that, contrary to what they expected, nobody opposed them, nobody resisted them, and that everything was left open and unguarded ... they took full advantage of it ... everyone set out to meet them carrying crosses and sacred icons as is the custom in processions and festivals. None of this helped to change their hearts. On the contrary, they mocked them, and this unhappy show did not lessen the horror and fury of their sack one little bit ... no one escaped the grief. In the streets and squares, in the churches there was moaning, weeping, wailing and lamentation, the groans of men, the howling of women. There was maiming, raping, imprisonment and the betrayal of those most dear ... There was no place that escaped the horror, there was no sanctuary for the fugitives. Every place, everywhere was crammed with every kind of terror ... The Saracens did not act in this way, but when they took Jerusalem they treated the people most humanely and with great mercy ... They did not make the way of the Holy Sepulchre a descent to Hell.'

The Attack on Constantinople

THE PLAN TO ATTACK CONSTANTINOPLE

The crusaders who made their own way to the east were in the minority. The majority decided to attack the city of Constantinople. The idea of attacking the city was not a new one, and given the background of resentment and misunderstanding over the past 100 years, the Byzantines did not seem to be real Christians. The leaders of the crusade persuaded the rank and file that this was the right course to take. Innocent was told only that the crusaders were going to restore the rightful heir to the Byzantine throne and that Alexius would then end the schism between the Latin and Greek churches. Unity between eastern and western churches was one of Innocent's prime aims, so he agreed to the expedition to Constantinople on condition that there was to be no attack on Christians.

ALEXIUS ANGELUS

The crusading fleet anchored in Constantinople in July 1202 and attacked part of the city. The emperor fled. The palace officials brought the old and blind Isaac Angelus from his prison cell and reinstated him on the throne. Alexius was then installed as co-ruler with his father in order to stop the fighting. Alexius tried to honour his promises to the crusaders but he was not successful. He could not raise the money he had offered, and there were not enough troops to supply any for the crusading army. He ordered the clergy to acknowledge the pope as the supreme authority in the church but they refused. In trying to honour his promises he alienated not only the crusaders but also his own people. The people of Constantinople, oppressed by taxes and harassed by the crusading army encamped outside the city, revolted in February 1204. They strangled Alexius and threw his father into a dungeon, where he died of grief. A nobleman by the name of Murzuphlus, who was known to be very anti-western, was made emperor.

THE SACK OF CONSTANTINOPLE

The crusaders now decided to put one of their own people on the Byzantine throne and divide the empire between them. They attacked from their warships: on 12 April 1204 they won control of the walls and by the following day they had taken the city. There followed three days of indescribable horror as the crusading army went through the city looting and massacring. No one and nothing was safe: priests and nuns were violated and killed, babies were smashed to pieces against walls, churches were ransacked and relics stolen to take back to the west. The glorious city of Constantinople, with its works of art collected over centuries, with its awe-inspiring churches and wealth of holy relics, was reduced to a smoke-blackened, bloodstained city of desolation.

A NEW LATIN EMPIRE

All thought of going to Egypt to fight against the Muslims was now abandoned. Instead, the crusader leaders set about systematically carving up the Byzantine empire into fiefs and sharing it between them. Baldwin of Flanders was elected emperor of the new Latin empire, but without the power of former Byzantine emperors. The Venetians gained a large part of the coast of the empire and three eighths of Constantinople. The Latin empire was not successful, however. The Greeks established a rival emperor at Nicaea and there were constant revolts.

When Innocent III first heard of the capture of Constantinople he was pleased because he thought that the two churches would be united. He wrote to congratulate Baldwin, approving of all that had been done. However, when he later heard of the massacre he was horrified. The damage had been done, however. To the Byzantines it appeared that the pope had blessed the destruction of their city and its inhabitants. This was unforgivable.

EPILOGUE

The crusade to Egypt to free the Holy Land had been abandoned. The Christians in the east who had called for their brethren in the west to help them against the Muslim invaders in 1095 had now been defeated, killed or scattered. The Byzantine empire had lost its lands, not won them back. The Latin states were hanging on to a narrow strip of land in the near east. The ideal was not quite dead – there were to be other crusades, including one by children in 1212. Jerusalem was to be regained by treaty in 1229 and lost again in 1244. The crusader states limped on until 1291, when the Mamluk Turks, the sons of the slaves who served the dynasty founded by Saladin in Egypt, destroyed their last outpost at Acre. The fourth crusade was, however, the last of the great international expeditions when the leaders of Europe united under the sign of the cross.

1. Complete the flow chart that you started on p. 46.
2. Answer the question: *Why did the crusaders attack Constantinople?*

Innocent III on the sack of Constantinople

'How is the Church of the Greeks, when afflicted with such trials and persecutions, to be brought back into the unity of the Holy See? ... it now abhors them [the Latins] as dogs. For they who are supposed to serve Christ rather than their own interests, who should have used their swords only against the pagans, are dripping with the blood of Christians.'

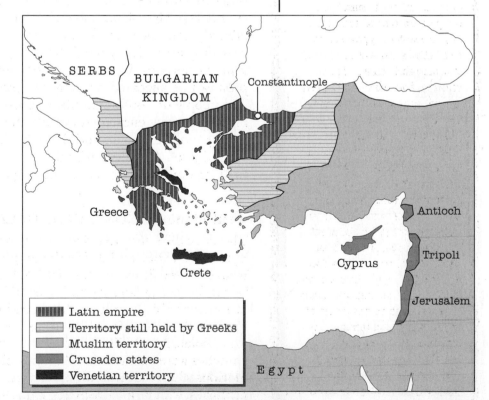

The eastern Mediterranean after the establishment of the Latin empire, c. 1205

Map legend:
- Latin empire
- Territory still held by Greeks
- Muslim territory
- Crusader states
- Venetian territory

Map labels: SERBS, BULGARIAN KINGDOM, Constantinople, Greece, Crete, Cyprus, Antioch, Tripoli, Jerusalem, Egypt

Synthesis: The Crusading Ideal

The ideals that people have reflect their beliefs, needs and aspirations. If we trace the development of the crusading ideal we will see how these changed throughout the crusading period. Changes do not happen in a vacuum: the ideals of the first crusaders affected events and the events of the crusades altered the ideal. By examining this interplay of ideals and events we will bring together, or synthesise, all that we have investigated in the previous chapters.

A PILGRIMAGE IN ARMS

At first, the crusade was considered to be a pilgrimage in arms. However, the success of the first crusade, against almost overwhelming odds, was interpreted as a divine seal of approval. The ideal that developed from this was that the crusade was a monastery at war. The supreme example of the ideal was the military orders, the fighting monks. Four phrases used in connection with monastic life also came to be seen as relevant to knights on the battlefield. These were: the knighthood of Christ, the way of the cross, spiritual warfare against the devil, and seeking for a heavenly Jerusalem. When we see how these phrases were used in the context of the first crusade it will help us to understand how the crusading ideal came to be shaped.

THE KNIGHTHOOD OF CHRIST

The idea that the actual rank of knight was important was shaped by the failure of the so-called 'people's crusade'. This expedition was almost entirely destroyed in Asia Minor and its failure showed that piety was not enough. It was the crusade of the knights that was successful. Christ wanted knights to fight his cause.

Knights, like monks, had to take a vow on entering their profession. The first step that the crusaders took at the start of their mission was to take a vow. Later, most of the knights took a vow to serve the interests of Alexius Comnenus, the Byzantine emperor. Many of the crusaders were idealistic: they gave loyalty and allegiance to Alexius as vassals to a lord. Alexius' actions during the crusade, however, may have led them to believe that he saw them only as mercenaries. Among the western barons there was not one overall commander. The knights must have thought that earthly leaders had let them down, but there were many visions and miraculous happenings, which proved that Christ himself was the leader. It was a short step from there to say that Christ himself had willed and directed the operation. The crusaders were literally the knights of Christ.

THE WAY OF THE CROSS

Jesus had said, 'If any man would come after me he must deny himself, take up his cross and follow me.' This was the way of salvation.

Penance

Penance was something that was imposed by the church to be done on earth, in order to show repentance for sin so that absolution (forgiveness) could be granted. Urban may have thought that taking part in the crusade was going to be so dangerous and uncomfortable that no further penance would be required by the church before all sins were forgiven. However, as most of the crusaders were not theologians they may have thought that going on crusade gained them complete forgiveness of sins. Historians debate this (see the detailed arguments in H. E. Mayer, *The Crusades*). Exactly what was meant by penance and remission of sin is very difficult to understand. Nevertheless, as the crusades progressed it became forgiveness of sins that was offered by the pope, rather than the opportunity to do penance for them.

The creators of the ideal

Monks began writing about the crusades after the capture of Jerusalem. We have to remember that our information comes from these people: religious, idealistic men, trained theologically, who interpreted the events happening in the world in the light of what the Bible said or what the church taught. They wanted to make sense of what was happening so that they could see how to please God. We do not know what the ideals of the peasants were. This was an extremely religious age and there was no education available outside of church circles. The writings of the monks represent, therefore, the interpretations of the educated people of the age.

The first crusaders stitched a cloth cross to their clothing, denied themselves and set out for Jerusalem to follow Christ. However, by going to war, the crusaders were putting themselves in a position of dying with their sins unforgiven on the battlefield. It is not clear what Urban II meant when he offered remission of sins; it may have been that the crusade was to be a sufficient penance for sins. However, the victories led people to believe that those who had died were martyrs in a just cause. Martyrs went straight to heaven. Visions of martyred saints reinforced this idea. If death in a crusade was martyrdom then to take part was a way of salvation.

The way of the cross in a monastery also implied brotherhood. The western crusaders had gone to the aid of their brethren in the east. The privations of the the march across Asia Minor were suffered by rich and poor alike. They were surrounded by enemies and could only look to each other for support. Monks also had to set themselves apart from sin, to fast and pray. The crusaders fasted and prayed and heard sermons before their battles. When they did this they were victorious. The message was clear and confirmed that monastic values were valid on the battlefield.

WARFARE AGAINST THE DEVIL

The idea of spiritual warfare against the devil became the ideal of physical warfare against the infidel. God intervened in his providence to show the crusaders that he approved of their mission by giving them victories, despite lack of numbers and lack of supplies, and by enabling them to take spoil from their enemies. This confirmed that God wanted the infidel to be killed. If killing the infidel for Christ could be seen as at Christian duty then it could be forgiven. The crusading knight did not die with his sins unforgiven on the battlefield.

THE HEAVENLY JERUSALEM

Just as the monks in their monasteries were seeking a heavenly Jerusalem, so the image of Jerusalem was a powerful one in the minds of those setting off on the first crusade. After the capture of Antioch, the leaders delayed but the rank and file forced them to press on to Jerusalem. The army that eventually reached the Holy City was vastly depleted and yet it was successful. God gave the city into their hands and they considered that, thereafter, it was their duty to hold it for him. Jerusalem, therefore, became a central tenet of the crusading ideal.

CONCLUSION: THE CRUSADING IDEAL

These ideas were only starting to take shape at the beginning of the first crusade, but were developed by its successes into the ideal of the monastery at war. The 12th-century theologians saw that the knight of Christ could be a real knight, the way of the cross could literally be to take a cloth cross and follow Jesus to Palestine, spiritual warfare could be physical warfare and the seeking for a heavenly Jerusalem could be equated with finding the earthly Jerusalem and putting its inhabitants to the sword. Therefore, the idea of serving in a crusade came to be seen as both heroic and religious, involving dedicated service to Christ in protecting the Christian world.

Idealism and warfare

It is very hard for us to think of idealism and warfare in the same context when our television screens remind us almost daily of the horror and futility of war. If we do think of idealism in war at all, perhaps it is in connection with giving life to defend democracy, or of a fair fight with both sides observing certain rules. It is more likely that our ideal is peace. This reflects our beliefs, needs and aspirations.

We have to remember that life in the 11th and 12th centuries was, in most cases, pretty horrific by our standards; warfare was almost a constant factor. There was no expectation of a life spent at peace. A life that would please God was the aspiration of many because they then had some hope of a better life after death. People looked for signs of God's pleasure or wrath. They were used to interpreting such things as the quality of the harvest or outbreaks of disease as signs of God's will. When Urban II proclaimed the first crusade, people cried out, 'It is God's will!' There is evidence that many who joined the crusades were idealistic: they sold or mortgaged their land in order to do what they perceived to be God's will.

A changing world

There were many changes in European society in the 11th and 12th centuries but it is not possible to examine them in detail in this book. Here is a brief list: you may like to consider how each of these changes might have affected the way in which people thought and acted, and therefore the way in which the ideals of the crusaders may have changed:

- The population grew;
- Towns and trade grew;
- Kings became stronger and developed more efficient systems of administration;
- The church was reformed;
- New monastic orders were created;
- The power of the pope increased;
- Heresy (belief in teachings contrary to the orthodox teachings of the church) became a problem that the church had to deal with.

A DEGENERATION OF THE IDEAL?

After the first crusade, the western knights took on the responsibility for the establishment of the Latin states. They tried to maintain a western European way of life in a land surrounded by enemies, in which they had neither sufficient forces to defend themselves nor means for independent economic survival. The Latin states became a peculiar concern of western Christendom. The second, third and fourth crusades were preached in response to problems that arose there. They saw a different type of crusader with a different style of leadership. The west was going to the rescue of its own, rather than to the aid of an eastern emperor. What was the crusading ideal now? Was it still the ideal of a monastery at war?

THE CHRISTIAN KNIGHT

Over the years, taking part in a crusade had become something that a knight was expected to do to prove that he was a Christian nobleman. The supreme examples of the knights of Christ, the Hospitallers and Templars, fought alongside the knights from the west on the third crusade. This should have been the crusading ideal at its height and yet there was now a major change: the military orders had come under the leadership of Richard I. Richard, rather than Jesus, was in control of victory or defeat.

In calling for the fourth crusade, Innocent III was anxious to get back to the ideal of knights, rather than kings, taking the lead. However, most of the knights did not reach the Holy Land because they were prevented by the actions of their leaders. If the ideal was still that they were knights of Christ, would they not have sacrificed all and trusted in his miraculous powers to get to the Holy Land?

THE IMPORTANCE OF FUNDING

The crusaders continued to take the vow and the cross, but the way of the cross was no longer the monastic way of poverty, chastity and obedience. The leaders of the third crusade, went to great lengths to ensure that they had sufficient funds to prosecute their wars. Both Richard and Philip Augustus levied a special tax. Innocent III levied a tax on the church for the fourth crusade, but lack of money was one of the biggest reasons for its failure to reach the Holy Land and for the consequences that followed. The crusaders could not envisage setting out on their journey only equipped with faith that God would provide. Ensuring that one was adequately funded became an important part of crusading.

THE REWARD OF SINS FORGIVEN

The promise of remission of sins given to the third and fourth crusaders should have supported the ideal that the crusade was the way of salvation. Innocent III declared an indulgence: that sins would be forgiven by God in return for taking part in a crusade. The emphasis was not on the penance that a man could do but on the reward a loving God would give to the faithful. According to Joinville, one of the fourth crusaders, 'because the indulgence was so great the hearts of men were much moved'. In this way, however, there was a movement away from the monastic ideal of continuous prayer and penance and towards an emphasis on reward.

BROTHERS IN ARMS

Many of the later crusaders had family who had settled in the crusader states. It was a family tradition that they should go, or they had family there who needed their help, or they had lands there which they hoped to gain or regain. This was an entirely different situation from that of the first crusade. There was no longer the idea of the isolated monastic brotherhood clinging to its members for support and fellowship while it fought against the enemies that surrounded it. Even amongst the kings, the sense of unity in a common cause was weak. Richard I had to cut short his campaign in order to get back to his lands in the west, as his brother John and fellow crusader Philip Augustus were conspiring to deprive him of them. After generations of misunderstandings and hostility, there was so little idea of brotherhood with the eastern Christians that the fourth crusaders were able to slaughter hundreds of them in Constantinople.

JERUSALEM

Just as the ideal of the heavenly Jerusalem had been strengthened by the capture of the city in 1099, so it was weakened by the failure to recapture it in 1187. Philip Augustus went home without even trying to get to Jerusalem; Richard I agonised and wept over it but decided not to try to take it as this would probably have meant the loss of the coastal towns, which were more important economically and politically. The secular had to take precedence over the religious. The fourth crusaders were diverted from Jerusalem and were content to have the riches and relics of Constantinople instead. The ideal of the heavenly city of Jerusalem was obviously degenerating.

CONCLUSION

The third and fourth crusades were not pilgrimages in arms going to Jerusalem to fulfil their vows: they were highly organised military expeditions. They were led by men, rather than by Christ himself. Their idea of brotherhood was with fellow western knights in Outremer. Money and commercial interests were a crucial element in deciding their course of action. The ideal of crusading had been realised in the establishment of the military orders. Crusading had been part of the warp and weft of knightly thinking for so long, however, that the ideal of a monastery at war with the infidel had degenerated. It had been replaced by the ideal of Christian chivalry at war with the enemies of the western church.

Try to answer the following question: *Was the degeneration of the crusading ideal inevitable?* You need to think about how changes in the medieval world affected different aspects of the crusades. Draw up a table, with the heading 'Areas of change' on the left, and 'First crusade', 'Second crusade' etc. across the page. In the left-hand column, the areas of change should include such things as the reasons for calling a crusade, method of finance, routes, relationship with the Byzantine empire and religious ideas. By filling in the table, you will be able to see in what areas there were changes after the first crusade.

For example, consider the changes in the forgiveness of sins promised to the crusaders. This promise became more definite and comprehensive as time went on. By the fourth crusade, it was being offered as a reward for taking part in the crusade.

You also need to address the following questions:

- The ideal of a monastery at war fulfilled a need at the end of the 11th century. Was that need still there at the end of the 12th century?
- Was the original ideal only something artificial that was created by the monk's interpretation of events, or did it really inspire knights to go to the east?
- Did crusaders continue to be inspired by the ideal or was their motivation increasingly materialistic?

In the synthesis section of this book we tried to bring together the issues involved in the crusades by tracing the development of a crusading ideal. Examination questions will test your understanding of these issues. They will also test your ability to answer the question in a structured way, by putting forward a convincing argument. A convincing argument puts points both for and against and comes to a reasoned conclusion. The purpose of this section is to help you to see how to work out your argument and structure your answer. The questions are of the type likely to be asked in an A-level examination.

Frequently exam questions ask if one factor was more important than the others in producing or contributing to a particular state of affairs. (See question 2 on this spread.) You will still need to analyse and write about *all* the factors involved, so it is advisable to decide first of all what factors were involved and sort out your information before going on to put the factors into their order of importance.

Factor – a group of events, actions and ideas linked by a common theme, such as religion, economy, society, individuals etc.

Argument

1. WHY WAS THERE SUCH AN ENTHUSIASTIC RESPONSE TO THE CRUSADING APPEAL IN 1095?

Why/how questions want you to analyse what happened and find the main factors that, in combination, give a full explanation of why events happened. The factors involved in the response to the crusading appeal were religious, social and economic. A table such as the one below is a useful tool to help you analyse your information.

Religious factors	Economic factors	Social factors
Appeal made on religious grounds: to help fellow Christians against the infidel	Younger sons did not have land: opportunity to gain land in the east	Feudal society geared up for war: a holy war allowed knights to stop fighting each other and combine against the infidel
Medieval man concerned about salvation: remission of sins offered	Poor harvests and growing population led to famine: peasants may have had little to lose by going	In some countries only the eldest son was allowed to marry and produce sons to inherit the land: crusades allowed younger sons to set up families in the east instead of entering a monastery
The importance of Jerusalem as the Holy City and the centre of the world Expectation of the end of the world: the earthly Jerusalem confused with the heavenly Vendetta to regain Christ's inheritance Religious motives shown by actions: they left all they had; few stayed in the east, but all went to Jerusalem		

Having broken down your information into key sections, you then need use it to form a structured answer. By analysing your information before you start you will avoid falling into the trap of using too much narrative. You are not being asked *what* happened but *why* it happened, so you have to take the events apart, as it were, to see what was behind them.

You then need to put your answer together in a logical way. Your answer will include an introduction, paragraphs explaining the religious, economic and social factors that combined to account for the enthusiastic response to the crusading appeal, and a conclusion.

2. To What Extent were Circumstances in the Muslim World Important in Determining why the First Crusade Succeeded and the Second Failed?

What you need to know

The events of the first and second crusades, the divisions within the Muslim world and the unifying work of Zengi and Nureddin.

How to work out your answer

You need to determine the reasons for the success of the first crusade and the failure of the second. To help you to work this out, try making a table with the first and second crusades as the headings. This will help you compare the different factors at work more easily.

A suggested answer plan

1. Introduction. The first crusade, without organised leadership, not financed properly, frequently close to starvation and extermination, succeeded against all the odds. The second, led by kings and well financed and organised, failed when it should have succeeded. There were many reasons for this.

2. Problems in Muslim world at the time of the first crusade: religious divisions and racial divisions. Leaders were away from cities, fighting each other, at crucial times. By the time of the second crusade Muslims had started to unite under Zengi and Nureddin against a common enemy. They were also inspired by the idea of the jihad.

3. The easy massacre of the first wave of crusaders had lulled the Muslims into a false sense of security. They had no knowledge of the western way of warfare and were horrified when they encountered the first charge of the knights at Dorylaeum. They did not underestimate the strength of the enemy in the second crusade.

4. The first crusaders had help from the Byzantines. Although this was never sufficient, it did enable them to continue at critical times. The second crusaders had no such help, as hostility had grown between Franks and Byzantines.

5. There was a strong sense of religious purpose and sense of unity amongst the crusaders in the first crusade. In the second, there were misunderstandings between the leaders from the east and the west, leading to the disastrous siege of Damascus. The monarchs from the west had no desire to settle in the Holy Land, and affairs in their own country hindered them. The Muslims had a stronger sense of religious purpose in the second crusade.

6. Conclusion. Circumstances in the Muslim world were partly the reason why the first crusade succeeded and the second failed. There were also other factors which changed between one crusade and the next. Weigh up the relative importance of these factors and come to your conclusion.

To what extent?

Many A-level questions begin with the words 'to what extent ...' These questions can be more difficult to answer than the 'what', 'why' or 'how' questions because they involve carefully weighing up the evidence and coming to your own conclusion. There is no right answer: the examiners want to see how well you can use a certain number of facts to argue a case. The secret lies in the thinking and planning, so you should try to get used to the idea of planning your argument before you start to write the answer.

Tables are a very useful tool for evaluating the evidence. When you are faced with a 'to what extent' question, divide your facts up into evidence for the different factors that you would identify for a why/how question. Then sort them into their order of importance. Why have you put them in this order? The answer to this will form the basis of your argument, so make notes on your table or add an extra column for this.

To sort out how important the various factors were in question 3, ask yourself questions such as: What might have happened if the defence of the Latin east had depended entirely on the military orders? How would they have managed without them altogether? Try to think of a scale line running from 'not at all' to 'completely'. Where on the scale line would you put the contribution of the military orders? How would you fill the rest of the space on the line so that a complete picture of the defence of the Latin states can be seen?

When working out your answer to question 4 you will first need to ask why the Latin kingdom of Jerusalem collapsed. Sort out the factors involved and then put them into two columns: those connected with the strengths of the opposition and those connected with the weaknesses in the kingdom. You can then decide more easily which you think was more important. You will still need to write about all the factors involved, but within the context of agreeing or disagreeing that the strengths of the opposition were more important. A good argument recognises the opposite point of view and explains why it is not accepted. (Remember: there is no right answer!)

3. To what Extent Did Defence of the Latin East Depend on the Contribution of the Military Orders?

What you need to know

How well defended (or fragile) were the crusader states in the east. Their dependence on the west. The role of the military orders.

What you need to write about

The difficulty in defending the Latin east. The importance of the military orders as a standing army. The disadvantages of the military orders. Other methods of defence such as castles, the tactics adopted and political manoeuvres, and their relative importance.

A suggested answer plan

1. Introduction. The security of the Latin east was always fragile from its foundation. There were never sufficient forces for defence. The states were surrounded by enemies on land and sea.
2. Owing to the relatively small numbers of knights in the Holy Land at any one time, the king lacked an army and resources to provide one. He was heavily dependent on the west. The military orders provided a permanent army, which protected pilgrims and guided them to Jerusalem.
3. The military orders brought in substantial wealth thereby not stretching the king's limited resources any more to pay them. They had a reputation as fierce fighters. They were committed, always in the thick of the battle and not scared to die. They were not ransomed if captured.
4. Defence also rested on castles built along eastern edge of Outremer. Many of these were controlled by the military orders. Defence from the sea was provided, at a cost, by the Italian trading cities. The kings developed a method of fighting which did not deploy all their forces in the field at one time. They also made strategic truces to enable them to conserve forces.
5. However, the military orders undermined the defence of the Latin east because they were independent and very wealthy. Their protection of Assassins' villages led them not to want peace treaties. Links with the west also undermined control of the territory. They supported rival factions in the claim to the throne. Eventually the style of recruit changed. They put the interests of their own order above that of the kingdom.
6. Conclusion. The crusader states could probably not have managed as long as they did without the military orders. To a large extent they were an important part of the defence of the Latin east, but they also undermined its defence in some ways, and there were other forms of defence available.

4. DID THE LATIN KINGDOM OF JERUSALEM COLLAPSE IN 1187–8 MORE BECAUSE OF THE STRENGTHS OF THE OPPOSITION THAN WEAKNESSES WITHIN THE KINGDOM?

What you need to know

The background of the situation in the Holy Land, especially the time prior to the battle of Hattin to the fall of Jerusalem in 1187; Saladin's unification of the Muslim world, and his army; the structure of the kingdom of Jerusalem and the disputes about the kingship.

What you need to write about

The strengths and weaknesses of the Muslim opposition; the strengths and weaknesses of the kingdom of Jerusalem.

A suggested answer plan

1. Introduction. The taking of Jerusalem by Saladin in 1187 followed the almost total destruction of the Frankish army at the battle of Hattin in the same year. This had come about largely because of divisions within the kingdom, which had left the Latin states with little military defence. Does this weakness, however, account completely for its fall?

2. The Muslims were in a strong position. Saladin's empire was at the height of its power. He was an extremely able commander who had a large army and troops motivated by religion. The battle of Myriocephalum in 1167 had virtually wiped out the Byzantine army, so the Franks could not call on them for help.

3. The kingdom of Jerusalem had never been secure but it had managed to hold on by adopting defensive tactics. If they had not been led to change this policy they would not have got engaged in battle at Hattin.

4. Saladin had to keep a Muslim army in the field for several years, and the strains were beginning to show. He had made a truce in 1185 in order to conserve his forces. It is possible that the Franks could have at least maintained their position had it not been for the crushing defeat at Hattin.

5. The kingdom of Jerusalem was weak because of squabbles over who should be king. There were two factions, one of largely Palestinian barons and the other of knights from the west. Reynaud de Chatillon broke peace treaties and attacked trade caravans. Muslims were supported by Syrian Christians. Had the Franks been less intolerant towards eastern Christians they would have had allies. Because of these divisions and different influences on King Guy, the Franks abandoned their policy of waiting and harassing the enemy and committed all their forces at Hattin, with disastrous results.

6. Conclusion. Weigh up the relative strengths and weaknesses. The Muslims were not as strong as perhaps it appears at first. They probably gained victory as much by the weaknesses and divisions within the kingdom of Jerusalem.

When you are deciding the order of importance of your factors, you will be selecting the evidence, weighing it up and interpreting it. When you write your answer, make your point in the first sentence of a paragraph and then use your evidence to substantiate, or back up, the point you have made. When you have finished your essay, read only the introduction, the first sentence of each paragraph and the conclusion, and ask if you have a complete answer to the question there in a nutshell. If you find that something seems illogical or has been repeated, try again. Then go back and read each paragraph. Ask yourself if the rest of the paragraph explains the point you made in the first sentence and makes it clearer. If you find sentences that are off the point, get rid of them or rewrite them.

The fourth crusade

Why the fourth crusade turned out to be so different from the three preceding ones is a key issue. Question 5 is asking you to examine the motives of the crusaders to see if there was a change over time. You will need to make a table similar to the one in the Synthesis section (page 53), with columns for motives in each of the crusades. Motives are extremely difficult to judge. You have to look at what was written, if anything, how the appeal for the crusade was put in order to inspire people to take part, and what they actually did that would confirm or deny the motives that you have inferred.

Introductions and conclusions

A good introduction sets the scene and opens up the subject for discussion. It need not be very lengthy. In your conclusion you should bring all the threads together, review your argument and say why you think as you do. Be wary of muddling up introductions and conclusions. Your introduction should not say what decision you have come to and your conclusion should not introduce any new factors.

5. WERE THE PARTICIPANTS IN THE FOURTH CRUSADE MORE INSPIRED BY MATERIAL CONSIDERATIONS AND LESS BY RELIGIOUS ZEAL THAN OTHER CRUSADERS?

What you need to know

The motives of the participants in the first, second, third and fourth crusades. The complications of the commercial interests of the Italian city states in the fourth crusade.

What you need to write about

Why people took part in the fourth crusade, contrasted with why they took part in the others. Religious, social and economic motives have to be considered and weighed up to see if the religious motive was of less importance in the fourth crusade than in others.

A suggested answer plan

1. Introduction. It is very difficult to assess what inspired any of the crusaders as the sources are few and far between. On the face of it would seem that the crusaders who destroyed Constantinople cannot have had the same religious zeal as those who had taken Jerusalem in 1099.
2. Motives were, from the first, mixed. Some of the first crusaders were going on crusade because of the failure of harvests, poverty and the desire of younger sons for land.
3. The second crusade was inspired by the loss of Edessa. Could this be seen as material? In preaching the second crusade Bernard of Clairvaux phrased his sermon along the lines of a business proposition. Louis VII may have gone to expiate his sin at Vitry sur Marne. Conrad did not intend to go but was overcome by the power of Bernard's preaching.
4. The kings going on the third crusade did not only have religious motives. Philip Augustus went to keep an eye on Richard. For both it was important to enhance their reputation as Christian warriors. Taxation for the crusade increased their power at home. Family and dynastic considerations were involved.
5. The fourth crusade was not lacking in religious motivation. It had been called by the pope. The crusaders were at the mercy of the Venetians because of lack of money. Enrico Dandolo took the cross. The pope had little control over actual events and condemned Christian attacking Christian. Some sources even say the crusaders attacked Constantinople for the relics. It was their deliberate decision to attack the city, however.
6. Conclusion. It is very difficult to assess motives, but we can judge them partly by the outcome. The first crusaders pressed on to Jerusalem and fulfilled their pilgrim's vows but some were rewarded with land. The second crusaders went to Jerusalem, the third sacrificed Jerusalem in order to keep control of the ports. In each crusade the religious and material motives were mixed.

Religious inspiration was not lacking at the beginning of the fourth, but events show that it was not strong enough to withstand the lure of the wealth of Constantinople. Decide for yourself whether or not this makes it less strong than in previous crusades.

6. TO WHAT EXTENT CAN THE EVENTS OF 1204 BE EXPLAINED IN TERMS OF EARLIER HOSTILITY BETWEEN LATINS AND GREEKS?

What you need to know about

You will need to know about the build up of hostility between Latins and Greeks since the first crusade, and the events of the fourth crusade.

What you need to write about

You will need to explain why the fourth crusaders sacked Constantinople, and to explain how these reasons were related to the hostility between the Latins and the Greeks and how they were related other factors, such as the influence of Venice on the course of events.

A suggested answer plan

1. Introduction. Eastern Christians spoke and had services in Greek, western Christians in Latin. There is a natural suspicion of those who are different, and this was present from the very start of the first crusade.
2. Bohemond caused suspicion and hostility. Alexius made the first crusaders take the oath, which was resented. The crusaders thought they had been betrayed by Alexius when he did not come to Antioch to help them and when he claimed the booty from Nicaea.
3. Manuel Comnenus was blamed for the ambush of Conrad's army in the second crusade. The Greeks were angry that no land had been given back to them after the first crusade. The capture of Cyprus was resented by the Greeks. Frederick Barbarossa was furious at his treatment by Isaac Angelus.
4. Another factor was the importance of Venice. The kings of Jerusalem had given Venice and other Italian cities tax concessions, which had led to trade rivalry with Constantinople.
5. Isaac Angelus and his dynastic ambitions were crucial. His inability to fulfil his promises to the crusaders caused hostility. The crusaders were frustrated, and they may have felt guilty about all they had done. Anti-crusader feeling in Byzantium spilled over and the sack took place.
6. Conclusion. The causes of the events of 1204 are extremely complex but to a great extent can be explained in terms of earlier hostility between Greeks and Latins.

Think long term and short term

The problem of the relationship between the Latins and the Greeks was an ongoing one throughout the crusades. To answer question 6 you need first of all to ask what happened in 1204 and why. Sort out your factors and then divide them into those that were long term and those that were short term. This will give you a much better idea of how things may have built up; it will also help you to see how factors that existed for a long time may have influenced the decisions taken in the short term. You can then assess their importance.

This is a difficult question to answer and requires a lot of hard thinking. Thinking, analysing and planning are essential parts of writing. At first it may seem that they take an awful long time but, with practice, you will speed up and it will certainly pay dividends in the quality of your answer.

'Throughout the crusades there had been a strange sense of fatality, a sense of doom. Even when the crusades were at their height, when the kings of Jerusalem appeared to be in full control, there seemed to be something wanting. Seen from the villages and cities of the West, Jerusalem appeared in men's eyes like a dream in shimmering Oriental colors, remote and inaccessible; and even those who walked through the streets of Jerusalem sometimes wondered whether they had really reached the place they had so desired to see. They had heard it called 'Jerusalem the Golden,' and they had imagined a city made of gold and rubies and emeralds. Instead, it was a dusty place, though the stones were the rich color of the crusts of bread. No city created by man could live up to Jerusalem's reputation. For two hundred years, proud men from the West fought a continuing battle for the city set on one of the mountains of the Judaean desert. For two hundred years, kings, princes, knights as well as the common people suffered from thirst and scorching heat to win and hold a city in the wilderness. Then at last they discovered that Jerusalem was not a geographical place. It was a place in the human heart.'

Robert Payne, The Crusades: A History, 1986

Final Review

THE END OF CRUSADING?

The crusading movement to the east did not end in 1204 but the fourth crusade was the last of the great international expeditions. In 1212 thousands of children followed a shepherd boy, who believed he had been chosen by God to lead a crusade, to Jerusalem. They thought that the Mediterranean would part, as the Red Sea had done for Moses, and let them walk to the Holy City on dry land. They were sadly disappointed and fell into the hands of pirates. Most of them either drowned or ended their days in slavery. However, this shows that the zeal for Jerusalem had not faded in the hearts and minds of ordinary people.

The fifth and subsequent crusades concentrated on attacking Egypt in order to enter the Holy Land from the south. Damietta was captured in 1219 but lost again two years later. The emperor Frederick II of Hohenstaufen recovered Jerusalem in 1229 by a treaty with the Muslims but he was under sentence of excommunication at the time and his kingship was not accepted. He had to leave the Holy Land. Jerusalem was lost again in 1244. The seventh and eighth crusades were led by Louis IX of France, later created Saint Louis, who died in Egypt of the plague. They, too, were a failure. The Latin states managed to survive because there were power struggles going on between the Ayyubids (the dynasty founded by Saladin in Egypt) and the Mamluks, their former slaves. The Latin states finally collapsed in 1291, after the capture of Acre by the Mamluks.

WHAT EFFECT DID THE CRUSADES HAVE ON THE WEST?

The idea of the church making war on its enemies took root in the west. Christians were urged by St Bernard of Clairvaux to 'fight the heathen until such time as, by God's help, they shall either be converted or wiped out'. Crusades against the heathen living to the north of Germany followed. The fourth crusade was closely followed by a crusade against the Albigensian heretics in southern France. In this case, Catholic knights fought against Catholic princes, who had allowed the heretics to live in their cities. The call to crusade by the pope was couched in the same terms as that of the crusades to the east: they were promised remission of sins and they could claim the booty. Popes had become strong because of their involvement with the crusades but, paradoxically, the papacy was weakened because it lost touch with the ideas and aspirations of ordinary men and women.

The crusades brought the feudal society of the west into contact and conflict with the great civilisations of Byzantium and Islam, but the everyday life of people in the west does not appear to have changed dramatically. Certain eastern products became popular, such as sugar, lemons, melons, lighter textiles and new colours from dyes, such as ultramarine. Castle building developed because of experiences with building castles in the east, and architecture developed because of contact with new ideas; relics were brought back to the churches to be cherished by local congregations; trade routes were opened up to the east, which led to further exploration, but the west resisted the philosophy, literature and scientific knowledge of the east.

The western nations did, however, become more aware of their nationalities. Having been united in a common cause, they learned to know one another better and to note, and hate, the differences between them. Monarchs were becoming stronger; taxing their subjects to pay for a crusade put them in an even stronger position, especially as they continued to levy the taxes even when a crusade was not planned. Loyalties to king and country developed. National pride was something new: previously men had thought of themselves primarily in terms of their religion. This was not entirely due to the crusades because social, economic and political changes were taking place all over Europe at this time, but the crusades acted as a catalyst to change.

WHAT EFFECT DID THE CRUSADES HAVE ON THE BYZANTINE EMPIRE?

The Greek and Latin churches had split in 1054. At the time of the first crusade there was hope of reconciliation. The crusades, however, brought the hostility between Greek and Latin churches out into the open. Constantinople was ransacked in 1204, its buildings destroyed and its treasures stolen. The Greek army finally recaptured it in 1261, 57 years after the creation of the Latin empire, but the Byzantine empire had been so severely weakened that it was never again to become a great political power. It survived for another 200 years and was finally destroyed by the Turks in 1453. The dukes of Moscovy then took over the role that the Greek emperor had played in the Greek Orthodox church and its centre moved to Moscow.

WHAT EFFECT DID THE CRUSADES HAVE ON THE WORLD OF ISLAM?

The inhabitants of Outremer had refused to be assimilated into the culture of the Islamic world. As a reaction to this, Islam itself became intolerant. Where once religious minorities, such as Syrian and Greek Christians, had been tolerated, now they were persecuted. The Turks, former slaves with a similar culture to the feudal west, rather than the Arabs, with their great, highly developed civilisation, dominated Islam. They tried to spread their religion at the point of a sword. In a time of warfare religious ideas cannot develop, but neither can prosperity. The Ottoman Turks, who succeeded the Mamluks, spread their domain across eastern Europe as far as Vienna, but poverty invaded the near east.

'The Crusade (or the idea of the Crusade) provided the young nations of the West with a common ideal and an apparently concrete and precise means of realising this ideal. This was only apparent because, consciously or unconsciously, it was always the celestial Jerusalem which lay at the root of all the Crusaders' sermons, speeches and ambitions. This kind of surge of mystical feeling in politics, in which material aspirations were overlaid with a veneer of mysticism, cannot be said to be unique in history, but rarely have the two motives been so perfectly fused.'

Zoe Oldenbourg,
The Crusades, 1965

'Above all, they [the crusades] reinforced the barriers between Christianity and Islam, poisoning relations in which Westerners were cast in the role both of aggressors and losers. In short, the Crusades brought Christianity into disrepute.'

Norman Davies, Europe: A
History, 1996

HISTORIOGRAPHY

There is a statue of Richard Coeur de Lion in the square outside the Houses of Parliament. It epitomises the image of the romantic, dashing, brave king who sallied forth for the glory of God and England to defeat the infidel. This is an image of Richard that was popular in the 19th century, when the statue was made – the days of the British empire, when Christianity was a missionary force and conversion to Christ often meant conformity to British ways and lifestyle. In those days the crusades were thought of as being a glorious episode.

Sir Stephen Runciman, who wrote his history of the crusades in the 1950s, concludes his work by saying that the crusades were 'nothing more than a long act of intolerance in the name of God, which is the sin against the Holy Ghost'. This is a very different point of view from that portrayed by the statue. Runciman was writing after a major war in which the world thought it had experienced the ultimate in atrocities and slaughter. More recently, historians such as Jonathan Riley-Smith have argued that it is possible to understand the crusaders without necessarily condoning their actions. This is because of modern movements, such as Christian Liberation in South America, which in the 1960s thought it right to use force to gain justice for the poor and the oppressed. Historians can only interpret the evidence that is left from the past, and they have to do it in the terms of the present that they inhabit. That is why views of the crusades have changed over time and, doubtless, will change again.

THE LEGACY OF THE CRUSADES

For better or for worse the crusades are part of our collective memory. We use the word 'crusade' to describe the action of people dedicated to a cause. There is a Christian youth group called the Crusaders. They have the crusader cross on their badge and they encourage young people to dedicate their lives to Christ. The St John's ambulance brigade continues the work begun by the Knights Hopitaller, again wearing the crusader cross on its badge.

There is a legacy, also, of ideas and attitudes. Conflicts in the name of religion are still among us: the problem of Northern Ireland illustrates this. East and west still misunderstand one another. At the time of writing the west is poised to attack Iraq becasue of its refusal to allow United Nations inspectors to view all its arms factories. As part of his political propaganda, Sadam Hussein, the leader of Iraq, had a poster made portraying himself, with his modern weapons, alongside Saladin with his horsemen. This was to evoke the idea of the great leader of Islam fighting the holy war against the infidel from the west.

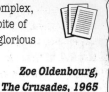

'... a long, complex, and yet in spite of everything, glorious adventure.'

Zoe Oldenbourg,
The Crusades, 1965

The state of Israel occupies much of the territory occupied by the Latin states. As a country, Israel has a definitive religion, different from its Muslim neighbours, and a fragile hold on its territory, which has constantly needed to be defended. Jerusalem is still a place of pilgrimage and a holy city for Christians, Muslims and Jews. Christians of eastern and western traditions are still divided. Christians of a certain belief still look to the Holy Land as being the place where Jesus Christ will come again. Some think that that time is not far away, as did the early crusaders.

CONCLUSION

Many of the incidents that occurred in the crusades are horrific and, to our minds, absolutely barbaric. We do, however, have to try to think ourselves back into the age in which they happened. Life was hard and, for most, short. Eternal salvation was of extreme importance; it is barely spoken of today. Warfare was a fact of life; today we try to use all means to avoid it. The king's government depended on his ability to win battles, not on his skill at the negotiating table. And yet in these days of negotiation, representation, democracy and a code of decency in public life, leaders of nations have extra-marital affairs, they argue and fall out and factions develop. In these 'enlightened' days there are still massacres of groups of people of different races and religions. Sometimes the euphemism 'ethnic cleansing' is used, but the equivalents of the massacres of the Jews and the slaughter of the people of Jerusalem and Constantinople are still with us today.

While the crusades cannot fail to horrify if we study them with any intensity, they also fascinate because of the range of human beings represented there. The key personalities seem to speak to us directly through sources that are uncomplicated by concerns about literary style. Although historians have condemned the crusades, and there is much in them to be condemned, they reflect much of what is still going on in the world today. The story of the crusades is the story of human beings with all their strengths, their weaknesses and their inconsistencies. The founder of Christianity, Jesus Christ, knew only too well the weaknesses of mankind and he predicted that 'there will be wars and rumours of wars'. There were wars when he walked the earth, there were wars when the crusaders walked in the places where he had trod and there are wars still. Our challenge is to enter into the distant world of the medieval age and try to see how faith and slaughter could go hand in hand. Perhaps, in trying to understand the world of the crusaders, we may learn to make a bit more sense of our own.

Index

Abbasid dynasty   7, 8, 17, 34, 35, 36
Acre   8, 9, 27, 40, 43, 44, 45, 49
Adhémar, bishop of Le Puy   22, 23
Aleppo   34, 36, 37, 40
Alexius Angelus   9, 47
Alexius Comnenus   6, 16, 17, 18, 22, 23, 24, 25, 50, 58
Amalric I   29, 33, 35, 36
Antioch   6, 24, 25, 26, 40, 42, 43, 51, 59
Arsuf   8, 32, 44
Ascalon   32, 33, 35, 44, 45
Assassins   32, 33, 36, 56

Baldwin I (Baldwin of Boulogne)   21, 22, 23, 24, 26
Baldwin II   26, 29, 31
Baldwin III   35, 37, 38, 47
Baldwin IV   29, 37, 44
Baldwin of Flanders   49
Bernard of Clairvaux   8, 9, 31, 38, 39, 41, 58, 60
Bohemond of Taranto   23, 24, 25, 26
Boniface de Montferrat   46
Byzantine empire   6, 10, 11, 16, 17, 18, 22, 24, 27, 36, 39, 43, 49, 61

Chansons de geste   21
Clermont   6, 18, 19
Conrad III   8, 38, 39, 40, 41, 58, 59
Conrad de Montferrat   43, 44, 45, 47
Constantinople   6, 9, 11, 16, 22, 39, 42, 45, 46, 48–9, 53, 58, 59, 61, 63
Courts in the Latin states   27
Crusading ideal   7, 10, 11, 30
Cyprus   43

Damascus   8, 27, 32, 33, 35, 36, 40, 41, 55
Doge of Venice   8, 9, 47, 58
Dorylaeum   6, 24, 39, 55

Edessa   6, 8, 9, 24, 26, 35, 38, 40, 58
Egypt   7, 9, 34, 35, 36, 37, 44, 45, 46, 49, 60
Eleanor, wife of Louis VII of France   40
Emich of Leisingen   22
Eustace of Boulogne   22, 23

Fatimid dynasty   7, 8, 17, 35
Frederick I (Barbarossa)   8, 42, 43, 59
Fulk of Anjou   38, 47

Godfrey de Bouillon   6, 22, 26, 30
Guy de Lusignan   29, 43, 44, 45, 57

Hattin   8, 9, 29, 32, 33, 37, 42, 57
Henry IV   14, 15, 22
Holy Roman emperor   6, 14, 16, 21
Holy Sepulchre   6, 26, 32
Hospitallers   (Knights of St John of Jerusalem)   7, 30–31, 32–3, 52, 56, 62
Hugh of Vermandois   22, 23, 25
Humphrey de Toron   44

Innocent III   8, 9, 46, 47, 48, 49, 52, 53
Isaac Angelus   42, 47, 48, 59
Italian cities   7, 11, 28, 37, 45, 46, 47, 56

Jaffa   44, 45
Jerusalem   6, 8, 9, 10, 11, 14, 17, 18, 19, 21, 23, 24, 25, 26, 35, 37, 40, 42, 44, 45, 51, 53, 57, 58
Jews   6, 22, 38
Jihad   7, 8, 34, 35, 55

Latin empire   9, 49
Latin states (Outremer)   6, 8, 10, 11, 26–7, 30, 32, 34, 38, 40, 41, 42, 52, 53, 56, 57, 60, 63
Leopold of Austria   43, 44, 45
Louis VII of France   8, 38–9, 41, 58
Louis IX of France   9, 60

Manuel I Comnenus   36, 39, 41, 46, 59
Melisende   29, 38

Nicaea   6, 24, 39, 49, 59
Normans   10, 14, 16, 18, 38
Nureddin   7, 34–5, 36, 40, 41, 55

Peter the Hermit   6, 18, 19, 22
Philip II (Augustus)   8, 42, 43, 45, 52, 53, 58
Pope   6, 7, 10, 14, 17, 18, 31, 32, 38, 41, 48, 60

Raymond of Antioch   40
Raymond de Saint Gilles, Count of Toulouse   23, 25
Reynaud de Chatillon   36–7, 57
Richard I (the Lionheart)   8, 11, 32, 36, 42, 43, 44, 45, 52, 53, 58, 62
Robert, Count of Flanders   22, 23
Robert (Curthose),   Duke of Normandy 15, 22, 23
Robert Guiscard   15, 16, 18
Roger of Sicily   15, 41

Saladin   7, 8, 9, 29, 35, 36–7, 42, 44–5, 62
Seljuk Turks   6, 9, 16, 17
Shawar   35, 36
Shi'ite Muslims   8, 17, 35, 36
Shurkuh   35, 36
Sicily   6, 10, 42, 43
Stephen, Count of Blois   22, 23, 25
Sunni Muslims   8, 17, 34, 35, 36

Tancred   23, 24
Templars (Knights of the Temple of Solomon)   6, 30–31, 32–3, 52, 56
Thibault, Count of Champagne   46
Tripoli   6, 26, 29, 42
Tyre   42, 43, 45

Urban II   6, 9, 15, 17, 18, 19, 20, 22, 38, 46, 51

Venice   7, 9, 16, 28, 46, 47, 49, 58, 59

Walter Sansavoir   22

Zara   9, 47
Zengi, atabeg of Mosul   7, 34–5, 38, 55